C000215601

Twentieth Century Architecture 4

Twentieth Century
Architecture 4

POST-WAR
HOUSES

The Twentieth Century Society
2000

TWENTIETH CENTURY ARCHITECTURE
is published by the Twentieth Century Society
70 Cowcross Street, London ECIM 6EJ

NUMBER 4 · 2000 · ISSN 1353–1964 · ISBN 0 9529 755 3X
Price £ 15.00. Orders by post please add £2 for postage and
packing (UK & Europe), £5 elsewhere.

The Twentieth Century Society was founded in 1979
as the Thirties Society to protect British architecture and design
after 1914.
Registered Charity No. 326746

Seven numbers of *Thirties Society Journal* were published between
1981 and 1991. *Twentieth Century Architecture* is the continuation of
Thirties Society Journal.
Previous volumes are
1. Industrial Architecture
2. The Modern House Revisited
3. Twentieth Century Churches

Editorial Committee:
Gavin Stamp, Elain Harwood and Alan Powers.
Guest editor: Tom Dyckhoff.
© The authors 2000

Designed and typeset in Quadraat
and Festival Titling by Dalrymple.
Printed by BAS Printers Ltd.

Contents

Acknowledgments

The Twentieth Century Society gratefully acknowledges its debt to the following generous benefactors to the Society who have enabled its work to continue and develop: R.W. Baker, Polly Beauwin, M.C. Bell, Brian Bloice, Derek Bottomley, Robert Bowles, Philip Bradley & Geraldine Kelly, Nicholas J. Bush, Elizabeth Casbon, Denis Clarke Hall, Miss J.M. Cleveland, Mr & Mrs N.J.S. Connor, Richard Constable, Dr Catherine Cooke, Mr & Mrs Roger Cooper, C.L. Don, Geoffrey & Susan Dudman, Mr & Mrs R.D.L. Felton, Mrs Wendy Franey, Deirdre Hicks, Peter N. Hirschmann, Trevor & Pauline Hucker, Brian Johnson, A. Kimpton, Jonathan King, Rhoda Lewis, Jack Lumley, Alison McKittrick, Miss H. McNie, Bruce MacTavish, Rick Mather Architects, Kenneth Mellon, Simon Morris, Steve Oddy & Paul Chamberlain, Wendy Paxford, Lynn F. Pearson & Sue Hudson, Juliet Penn-Clark, Sandy Rattray, Jane Riches, Mr & Mrs Rubens, Terry J. Scragg, Derrick Shorten, Katherine Sorrell, Alison Starling, Michael J. Stevens, Neil Taylor, Aidan Turner Bishop, The Lady Vaizey, J.R. Wall, John & Barbara Weeks, John Wibberley, Ms Gillian E. Wilson, Ralph Miles Wilson, Mr & Mrs Brian Woodcock.

The following have contributed towards the cost of the Society's current research on Post-War Social Housing: Baylight Properties plc, Donald Buttress, Terry Farrell & Partners, Feilden Clegg, Nicholas Grimshaw & Partners, The Manifold Trust, Marley plc, Richard Rogers Partnership, Sidell Gibson Partnership, Strutt & Parker.

The Society gratefully acknowledges the grant received from the Department for Culture, Media and Sport (and after April 2000 from English Heritage) for part of the cost of its casework.

1 Building Sight: House, London NW3 by Brian Housden

PAUL OVERY

Building Sight: House, London NW3 by Brian Housden

PAUL OVERY

AS a London suburb favoured by 'advanced' intellectuals and liberal-minded professionals, Hampstead was one of the few places in Britain where a handful of Modernist houses were built in the 1930s. It was also the site of some significant Modernist domestic architecture of the post-war decades. By this time and in such a location one might have expected Modernism to be accepted without comment and controversy. However, this was not entirely so, and No.78 South Hill Park was – and continues to be – a controversial building in its neighbourhood.[1] One reason for this may be that the house occupies a crucial position in an enclave of post-war architecture – within a larger area of late nineteenth-century speculative housing – that includes a well-known block of six terraced houses designed in the mid-1950s by William Howell, Gillian Howell and Stanley Amis (of the practice Howell, Killick, Partridge & Amis) for themselves and four clients.

No.78 South Hill Park must be seen (in part at least) as a confrontational design.[2] It sets its cap against not only the inflated grandiosity of the original Victorian houses, with their sub-Ruskinian, imitation-stone, pseudo-Venetian detail, but also the LCC Architects' Department 'received wisdom' of the Howell, Killick, Partridge & Amis terrace, the cottagey, 1950s 'Modernist vernacular' of the low-lying semi-detached villas in South Hill Park Gardens diagonally opposite it (unkindly described, during an unsuccessful campaign to save these from demolition in the late 1990s, as 'policemen's houses'), and the penny-plain, self-effacing 'in-fill Modernism' (constrained by the building regulations and shortages of the immediate post-war period) of the five-storey terrace house next door to No.78, designed by Alexander Gibson in 1948–1949. No.78 South Hill Park could be seen to subvert and challenge not only the consensual architectural ideas of the immediate post-war decades, but also the sentimental nostalgia that has been projected during this period and subsequently onto speculative Victorian housing.

THE EVOLUTION OF THE HOUSE

Brian and Margaret Housden began to search for a plot on which to build in the mid-1950s, after post-war building controls were lifted. They first looked at three derelict Georgian cottages in Cardinal Cap Alley, near Sir Christopher Wren's house at Bankside, opposite St Paul's. The site was spectacular but involved demolishing the cottages.[3] Two bomb sites in the Charlotte Street area, 40 Frognal, just above the house designed by Connell, Ward and Lucas in 1938, and two further bomb sites in South Hill Park were also considered. At the time, the plot on which No.78 was to be built belonged to John Killick, of Howell, Killick, Partridge & Amis, who planned to build a house on it for himself. However, Killick decided not to build on the plot and sold it on to the Housdens in the late 1950s.

In Housden's first plans and elevations submitted for planning permission in 1958, the reinforced concrete frame was exposed but did not continue to the level of the roof, which was a double monopitch quite different from the 'upturned

1. Dates and details of design and construction are based on two interviews with Brian Housden on 12 and 14 December 1998, and on a number of subsequent conversations. Views or paraphrased statements attributed to Housden are also based on these sources, unless otherwise stated.

2. No.78 South Hill Park has not been fully documented previously. Brief references to it appear in Kenneth Frampton's 1966 essay on the Maison de Verre (see note 32), and in Christopher Wade (ed.), *The Streets of Belsize*, London: Camden History Society, 1991, p.87, where it is claimed the house "has been variously called 'daringly brutal' and 'a ruined Japanese town hall'" (no sources are given for these comments). There is a short entry in Edward Jones and Christopher Woodward, with photographs by William Harrison, *A Guide to the Architecture of London*, London: Wiedenfeld & Nicholson, 1982, p.52.

3. The Goldfinger House in Willow Road (towards which No.78 South Hill Park looks across Hampstead No.1 Pond and East Heath) was built on the site of three Georgian cottages which Goldfinger had demolished.

figure 1
The garden front of No.78 South Hill Park, seen from Hampstead Heath.

tray' of the built design, integral with the structural frame. The front, rear and side elevations were infilled with brick, while the window frames and subframes were of wood.

According to Housden, this design was abandoned after a trip to the Netherlands in the late 1950s, when he and Margaret Housden visited the Rietveld Schröder House in Utrecht. Here they met Truus Schröder and Gerrit Rietveld, who lived at the house after the death of his wife in 1958 until his own death there in 1964. After driving the Housdens to Utrecht station, Rietveld asked Housden to send him plans for No.78 South Hill Park. On returning to London, Housden looked at the drawings he had submitted for planning permission and realised

figure 2
The street front of No.78 South Hill
Park.

4. Housden claims that he "substituted a far superior and more expensive twentieth-century European architectural design" in place of a "cheap conventional design in the mediocre twentieth-century English cultural tradition" (Notes sent to the author, April 1999). The design as built cost three times as much as the first design.

5. The English architect Edward Cullinan claimed in his address at the memorial meeting for Van Eyck in March 1999 that "Brian Housden, after a disastrous architectural education at the Architectural Association School of Architecture visited Holland and returned a mature architect". The memorial meeting was held in Van Eyck's last building, the National Audit Office, Lange Voorhout, The Hague, on March 12, 1999.

6. Glass blocks – rather than lenses – were used for the roof lights, which provide illumination for the landing at the top of the internal staircase. Glass blocks are formed from two pieces of bonded glass and are hollow inside. Unlike glass lenses, they can be used flat or horizontally.

7. "In the late 1950s, glass blocks suffered a major image problem, when they were nowhere to be found except in strictly utility use (prison cells proved popular)", (Miriam Cadji, 'Glass act', RIBA Journal, vol.106, no.6, June 1998, p.64). This applied equally to glass lenses.

their inadequacy.[4] On the same trip to Holland, the Housdens also visited Aldo van Eyck's Orphanage in Amsterdam (then nearing completion) where they met Van Eyck on site. Housden regards the impact of this building as being of almost equal importance as the Rietveld Schröder House to the final design of No.78 South Hill Park.[5]

The new design evolved between 1958 and 1963 and building began in October 1963. In the built design, hollow clinker concrete blocks faced with Venetian white glass mosaic and assemblies of glass-lens and reinforced-concrete panels were used to clad the elevations in place of the brickwork. Narrow strips of steel Crittall windows replaced the wood-framed windows of the first design. The house has been in continuous occupation by the Housden family since 1964. The interior is still in the process of completion and, not surprisingly, there have been certain changes and modifications to the house – mainly to the interior – over 35 years. However, it essentially remains located in the period when it was designed. Housden argues that it represents "an architectural statement in the twentieth-century European cultural tradition". A number of the major architectural components of No.78 were conceived as revised versions of the Modernist experiments of the late 1920s and early 1930s, in particular the panels of Nevada glass lenses set in reinforced concrete frames which are used in the cladding of the front and rear elevations.[6] Glass lenses or blocks were far from fashionable as a material when the house was built,[7] being generally confined to factories and municipal buildings.[8] Although they returned to fashion for interiors during the final decade of the twentieth century, their use for exterior walls or windows remains unusual.[9] The Maison de Verre in Paris of 1929–31 is the best-known historical example.

The site is very unstable. When the Hampstead Ponds were dug out in the eighteenth century, as a series of reservoirs to provide water for central London from the bed of the River Fleet (which rises about half a mile higher up on Hampstead Heath), large amounts of excavated clay were deposited on top of the existing topsoil, which itself lay immediately above London clay. A number of small underground streams flow down from Parliament Hill and South Hill into the Hampstead Ponds, running under the foundations of many of the houses in the street. A specialist company, Cementation, was engaged to assess the soil situation, and advised that piles should be driven to a depth of twenty feet below the level of the bottom of Hampstead No.1 Pond (i.e. about 40 feet deep in total). No.78's structural consultant, Niels Lisberg (the Danish engineer who taught at the Architectural Association when Housden was a student in the 1950s), disregarded this advice and instead specified a solution for the substructure that cost the same as driving 40-foot piles. This consisted of large concrete ground beams, reinforced with a ton of mild steel, to form a raft that supported the concrete post and slab superstructure, which contained five tons of high-tensile steel reinforcing rods. The concrete raft is cantilevered over the footings of No.76, remaining entirely independent of the neighbouring structure.[10]

THE HOUSE'S RELATIONSHIP WITH ITS SITE

The house's provocative relationship with its site may be divided into its relationship with its immediate urban context, and its relationship with the natural context – the Heath. Unlike the Howell, Killick, Partridge & Amis terrace, which may be seen as 'respecting' the English urban vernacular tradition of the original Victorian houses in the street, and the 'rue corridor' denigrated by Le Corbusier,[11] No.78 South Hill Park ignores the scale and 'social relationship' to one another of the neighbouring buildings, deliberately subverting their norms. This is apparent, for example, in the way that the concrete canopy over the garage space or car port projects provocatively beyond the building-line of the Victorian street, and in the recently-added (and subsequently removed) black-painted, industrial-style steel gates, which evoked considerable local opposition.[12]

When built, the house's plot faced a pair of large double-fronted, semi-detached 1870s Victorian houses, of the type that makes up most of the original housing stock in South Hill Park and South Hill Park Gardens.[13] To the left of these, diagonally opposite No.78, were a pair of 'vernacular-Modern', two-storey semi-detached houses of 1952 (on the site of two bombed Victorian houses), which were demolished in 1999.[14] Although it replaced the last in a row of four five-storey terrace houses, No.78 South Hill Park is both visually and structurally separate from the two surviving Victorian houses, and the immediately adjacent Gibson house of 1948–9 (No.76). Housden did not use the party wall of the latter when designing his structure, but made the reinforced concrete frame, and the raft which supports it, independent of No.76.

Housden made no attempt to merge the flat roof – which takes the form of a massive reinforced concrete 'tray' – actually or visually with the slightly higher roof levels of the Howell, Killick, Partridge & Amis terrace or the considerably taller Gibson house. The discrepancy of roof levels is more disturbing at the front of No.78, seen in foreshortened perspective from the street, than it is at the back when viewed from across the pond. Housden himself was later to design a penthouse conversion for the top floor of the Gibson house, incorporating very large plate-glass windows at the rear and two converging monopitch roofs.[15] It is interesting that Housden's first design for his own house had a double-monopitch

8. For the association of glass blocks or lenses with public lavatories in the 1950s, see Simon Ofield 'Consuming Queerspace: Deconstructing the Glass Brick Wall', Architectural Design, vol.68, no.1/2, January 1998, pp.58–51.

9. "Promoted as architecturally sexy, all negative associations [of glass blocks and lenses] have been successfully reversed", (Cadji, 1998, op.cit., p.64).

10. The reinforced concrete frame and raft were constructed by Sims & Russell Ltd.

11. Sherban Cantacuzino 'Introduction', to Howell, Killick, Partridge & Amis: Architecture, London: Lund Humphries, 1981, p.14. This row of standardised middle-class housing is often described as Le Corbusian. However, it almost certainly owes as much to the row of five four-storey, middle-class terraced houses with integral ground-floor garages in Amsterdam designed in 1937 by Mart Stam, Lotte Beese, H.A. Maaskant and Willem van Tijen.

12. Gates were shown in two of the three planning permissions obtained in 1958, 1962 and 1963. They were not erected until 1995, when it became clear that the forecourt of No.78 would be respected by neither dogs nor men.

13. South Hill Park was built in the form of a tennis racket. The oval in the middle, originally a communal garden, was soon built upon to form South Hill Park Gardens. The houses, which were erected in the 1870s, were described a hundred years later as "inelegant, tightly packed, and tasteless for such a fine situation; but no worse than most other unambitious middle-class suburban housing of the period" (F.M.L. Thompson, Hampstead: Building a Borough, 1650–1964, London: Routledge and Kegan Paul, 1974, p.307). A quarter of a century later it is difficult to disagree with this judgement.

14. These were replaced by a block of four five-storey speculators pastiche Victorian terrace houses fairly closely based on the original housing stock.

15. The conversion was carried out by the owner, not to Housden's specification.

16. These drawings date from 1958.

17. The inside and outside surfaces or the reinforced concrete panels into which the glass lenses are cast are painted in standard white Snowcrete concrete paint. This tends to make the concrete 'framing' less obvious and emphasize the glass lenses.

18. Glass lenses (unlike glass blocks or bricks) are a single thickness of glass. The Siemens Nevada obscured clear glass lenses used at No.78 South Hill Park are 3cm thick and 18cm square, with a circular indentation or 'lens' in the centre. The outer surface has an apparently 'random' amorphous pattern which renders the lens partially obscure.

19. The strips of standard, steel Crittall windows are cast into the reinforced concrete frames in a similar manner to the Siemens clear glass lenses.

20. The concrete and glass lens panels were also employed for the top lights of the projecting bay, but proved unsatisfactory in horizontal use. These have been replaced by plyglass.

21. Adolf Rading, 'Erläuterungsbericht' (Explanatory project notes), reprinted in Adolf Rading, Bauten, Entwürfe und Erläuterungen, edited by Peter Pfankuch, Berlin: Schriftenreihe der Akademie der Künste Vol.3, 1970, p.68, quoted in English translation in Auf dem Weg zum Neuen Wohnen: die Werbundsiedlung Breslau 1929/Towards a new kind of living, Basel, Boston, Berlin: Birkhäuser Verlag, 1996, p.24.

22. The slightly later Victorian houses higher up the street overlooking No.2 Pond, however, have bay windows at the rear.

23. Thompson, 1974, op. cit., pp.307–308. Another reason for the houses facing inwards would have been the original communal gardens in the centre of the oval at the top of South Hill Park (see note 13).

24. Since 1860 the Hampstead Junction Railway, which formed part of the North London Railway, provided cheap and quick access from Kingsland, Hackney, Homerton and Haggerston to Hampstead Heath station (situated at the bottom end of South Hill Park) for the working-class East Londoners who flocked to the Heath in their hundreds at weekends and in their thousands on Easter, Whitsun and August Bank Holidays, when three fairs were held on the Heath, the largest

roof, which in the surviving drawings gives the appearance of 'blending' with the neighbouring buildings.[16] By contrast the roof as built is one of the more 'transgressive' and uncompromising features of No.78 South Hill Park.

From the street side the massive reinforced-concrete frame appears to dominate the exterior. This effect is emphasised by the wide concrete roof-slab and cantilevered canopy above the garage-space or car port. At the rear of the building, on the other hand, the glass-lens and concrete panels are more clearly perceived as forming a screen wall than at the front of the house, especially when viewed from the Heath across the water of No.1 Pond.[17] However the contrast between the apparent opacity (from the outside) of these panels and the glinting combination of transparency and reflectivity of the rear windows of the neighbouring houses is particularly marked in juxtaposition to the wall-to-wall windows of the Howell, Killick, Partridge & Amis terrace.

The house seems to refuse the spectacular and picturesque qualities of its wider site, the much-admired views across Hampstead Heath and the Ponds. The use of obscured glass lenses set in reinforced concrete panels for the exterior rear elevation, in marked contrast to the large sheets of rolled glass in the panoramic bay-windows of the Victorian houses higher up the street, and the wall-to-wall, plate-glass 'picture windows' of the Howell, Killick, Partridge & Amis terrace, appears deliberately wilful.[18] Yet, look closer, and the long strips of shallow, steel-framed Crittall windows which divide the panels of clear glass lenses horizontally, actually provide surprising and exciting glimpses of water and landscape, producing a new and stimulating relationship between interior and exterior space, and the perception of this from within the house.[19] Rather than the 'controlling' perspectival viewpoint of the 'picture window' or Le Corbusian pan de verre, the house proposes different and more ambiguous viewing positions, those of the seated, or recumbent contemplative figure (for whom the narrow bands of Crittall windows set between the panels of opaque glass lenses are placed at the optimum height), or the inhabitant moving through the house. From the master bedroom, with its shallow rectangular bay cantilevered out beyond the line of the rear elevation (also clad with glass lens and concrete panels above a waist-height strip of Crittall window),[20] tantalising glimpses of the Heath can be seen from a sitting – although not easily from a standing – position, providing perceptions of difference and surprise. For the inhabitants of the house, moving through its different levels, sudden and unusual views of the Heath and Ponds are caught through the narrow bands of windows. Adolf Rading's comments on his own 1929 Breslau Werkbundsiedlung apartment block, seem strikingly appropriate to No.78 South Hill Park:

"Each apartment, on principle, is fitted with some windows that grant a view of the ground and cut off the view of the sky and some windows that offer sky but not ground vistas. The singular tension inherent in the appearance of this window-shape in the façade has its counterpart in the psychological tension of living (in this house) in that the conscious inclusion of sky and earth into one's living space will awaken the feeling that one's residence is related to vastness, to immensity."[21]

As such, the house actually has a dynamic relationship with the Heath, in marked contrast with its Victorian neighbours. This must relate to the difference in the popular perception of the Heath in late-Victorian and post-war London. Only a few of the neighbouring Victorian houses were built with bay windows at the rear,[22] and their back walls are a hotchpotch of non-matching windows and trailing down-pipes, typical of most non architect-designed houses of the period. In his history of Hampstead, Professor F.M.L. Thompson, has argued that in the development of the street during the 1870s as a 'lollipop' or tennis racket shaped cul-de-sac by the landowner Thomas Rhodes:

"The real crime was to make the whole estate inward facing to his dismal oval, so that the houses turned their ugly backsides to the Heath like so many rude apes. Quite apart from the pain inflicted on the sensitive walkers on the Heath, it showed a total lack of imagination and complete indifference to the locality; a piece of standardised routine suburbia was slapped down without a thought when houses turned outward with the fronts to the Heath would have fetched more as well as looked better."[23]

However, this account projects late twentieth-century sensibilities onto Victorian developers. To the bourgeois householder of the 1870s, Hampstead Heath would not have been seen as a particularly attractive and picturesque open space, but rather as a place of threat and danger to his family and property and as a site of confrontation.[24] To the class-conscious Victorian bourgeois, Hampstead Heath was a place to be viewed with caution and walked over only with circumspection. Not surprisingly, when built the Victorian houses presented their ornate and pompous frontages not to the Heath but to the street.

By the 1950s, however, after having declined further into multi-occupation and criminal association,[25] South Hill Park was beginning to undergo a process of gentrification by some of the more adventurous of the traditional middle classes, who saw the potential of what were now perceived as spectacular views and close access to desirable open spaces. The building of No.78 coincided with and was part of this process.[26]

MODELS OF DOMESTIC LIVING: THE MAISON DE VERRE AND THE SCHRÖDER HOUSE

The Rietveld Schröder House and Pierre Chareau and Bernard Bijvoet's Maison de Verre, with its exterior walls of glass lens and reinforced concrete panels, were the two 'iconic' Modern Movement buildings Housden visited and studied before completing his design.[27] When he visited the Maison de Verre, Housden noted that many of the glass lenses had cracked over a period of 30 years, due to the thinness of the reinforced concrete in which they were set, and the way in which the reinforcing rods had been enclosed within the concrete. At No.78 South Hill Park, three-centimetre thick Nevada clear glass lenses were cast into lightweight, reinforced-concrete frames set in aluminium mullions. The panels were vibrated after casting to eliminate air pockets.[28] Thirty-five years after installation, they appear to be still in good condition. Housden also noted that the Nevada glass lenses at the Maison de Verre, made by the French firm of Saint Gobain, had a greenish tinge, whereas he wanted to use the purest clear glass lenses then available. At the time, only the German glass manufacturer, Siemens, made clear Nevada lenses, and these were obtained from the English company that imported them.[29]

and most accessible of which was – and still is – located immediately across the ponds from South Hill Park. In addition South End Green was the terminus of the London Street Tramway Company and a number of horse bus routes, which also served to bring weekend visitors to the Heath from some of the poorest and most deprived areas of London. This was no doubt one reason why South Hill Park quickly fell into multi-occupation in the early decades of the twentieth century. After the Second World War, however, better off working-class Londoners began to afford cars and motorbikes, and to spend their weekends at the South Cast and their summer holidays in Spain.

25. In 1954 Styllou Christophi murdered her German daughter-in-law at No.11 South Hill Park and burnt her body in the back yard. She was the penultimate woman to be hanged in Britain. Ruth Ellis, the last woman to be hanged in Britain, shot dead her lover David Blakeley outside the Magdala public house at the bottom of South Hill Park in 1955.

26. Which brought its own irony. No.78's 'industrial' appearance caused a good deal of outrage and consternation at the time. This was exacerbated by the fact that for several years the house remained in an obviously very unfinished state with temporary wooden-batten and polythene exterior walls while Housden fought with the LCC district surveyor for permission to put up the concrete and glass lens panels. More recently, similar outrage ensued when Housden erected black steel gates in front of his house in the early 1990s. These were dismantled after a court order in February 1999, and at the moment of writing their future is uncertain.

figure 3
Elevation of the street front of the orginal design for No.78 South Hill Park, with its pitched roof.

figure 4
The latest addition to the house, the front gate and screen, added in the 1990s.

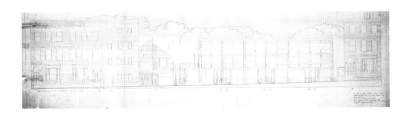

The structure of No.78 South Hill Park, clearly visible on the exterior, is closely linked to the formal organisation of the interior. The deliberate change of scale embodied in No.78, or rather its refusal to relate to the scale of the surrounding buildings – the scale of the house seems to refer entirely to itself[30] – and its repudiation of the 'inflated' proportions of the Victorian houses which make up most of the street, perhaps owe something to the way in which the Rietveld Schröder House similarly abuts a bulky terrace of overscaled 'traditional' brick-built suburban neighbours, and looks strangely small beside these, challenging its neighbours with its oddity and difference.

However, although the design of No.78 South Hill Park shows a careful study of these two major models, the predominance of exposed concrete as a material, and the massiveness of the structure, make the house very different from both, and locate it very much in the particular period when it was designed.[31] The Schröder House and the Maison de Verre were only just becoming known in the late 1950s in Britain,[32] where the influence of Le Corbusier had long been dominant – or at least was the only influence generally acknowledged by architects who wished to be considered Modernists.[33] Nevertheless, Housden claims that, inevitably, Le Corbusier was also an influence on the design of the house. This can be perhaps seen in the reinforced concrete frame structure, which is a sophisticated adaptation of the Maison Domino system. The reinforced concrete suspended staircase in the centre of the house is structurally independent of the main reinforced concrete frame,[34] relieving the post-and-slab structure from unacceptable stresses, and making possible the open plan of the semi-basement living/dining/kitchen area.[35] The visual disjunction that follows from its structural separation seems to give a springiness and flow to the space as perceived and experienced from inside that belies the massiveness of the frame.

In the manner in which it allows – or does not allow – views from inside to outside, the house is both similar and dissimilar to its two models. When Rietveld and Schröder chose the site and worked together on the design of the Schröder house in 1924, they finally settled on a plot at the end of a newly built road, orientating it so that the view from the main first-floor living and dining areas was across the open countryside of polders and dykes. However, they seemed to have wanted the house to combine the qualities of being both a house in the city and a house on the edge of the country. The view was best experienced (and most photographed) from the dining table at which Truus Schröder and her three children sat down to eat, which was the centre of family life in the house. However, the wide windows were fitted with blue half-blinds, which could be lowered to obscure the view, but still admit much light through the upper part of the windows. The most famous photograph of the interior of the house as inhabited space shows Schröder and her young daughter Han sitting at the dining table with their backs to the view, returning with a penetrating female gaze that of the camera and the photographer. Within a few years of its occupancy the open countryside disappeared as the polders were built upon. In the 1960s a raised motorway was constructed about twenty feet from the Schröder house.[36]

The Maison de Verre was built inside the courtyard of a typical Parisian *hôtel particulier*. The clients were a successful gynaecologist and his wife, Jean and Annie Dalsace. The house looks onto the interior of the courtyard and the small garden. As at No.78 South Hill Park, long strips of steel window are inserted between large areas of glass lenses. According to Housden (who interviewed Mme Dalsace when he visited the house in the late 1950s), it was her suggestion that the strips of clear glass window in the patients' waiting room were placed at a level where the women who had come to consult Dr Dalsace could not see the Dalsaces' children playing in the garden.[37] Mme Dalsace thought this might distress many of the patients who were having difficulty in conceiving. The lenses would freely admit light into the waiting room, but partially obscure the view into

27. Kenneth Frampton wrote of the Maison de Verre: "Traces of its syntax may be found in recent English buildings; works as diverse as James Stirling's Leicester Engineering Laboratories or Brian Housden's own residence in London", (Kenneth Frampton, 'Maison de Verre', *Arena: The Architectural Association Journal*, vol.81, no.901, April 1966, p.262).

28. The welded reinforcing rods were ⅛ inch thick. On the recommendation of the Aluminium Development Corporation, the mullions were made from sulphur-resistant marine aluminium alloy extruded sections with a high aluminium content, assembled by Housden. The mullions are regularly treated with Aerowax, developed to resist the oxidation of the surfaces of aluminium alloys in aircraft.

29. Healeys.

30. There are internal changes of scale in the interior. The ceiling height in the master bedroom is twelve feet, and in the three other bedrooms eight feet. This, like other aspects of the internal planning of the house, is reminiscent of Adolf Loos's notion of *raumplan*.

31. Comparable perhaps to the 1960s work of Ernö Goldfinger, the LCC Architects Dept designs for the South Bank, or the later National Theatre by Denys Lasdun. But the use of exposed concrete structure was unusual for a small house.

32. Housden regards these two houses as the most significant examples of twentieth-century, European domestic architecture. Kenneth Frampton claims the two "have much more in common beside their dependence upon an almost symbiotic relation of architect and client" (Frampton, 1966, *op. cit.*, p.257).

33. See Adrian Forty, 'Le Corbusier's British reputation', in *Le Corbusier: Architect of the Century*, exhibition catalogue, London: Hayward Gallery, the Arts Council of Great Britain, 1987, pp.35–41.

34. Cf. Le Corbusier's first unexecuted design for the Villa Baizeau (1928–29), near Carthage.

35. Because the house is built on a slope, the ground floor at entrance level is at first-floor level at the rear; the semi-basement at the front opens onto the garden at the rear.

the garden. Because an elderly sitting tenant on the top floor of the existing build-ing refused to move, the new house was inserted underneath this – a construc-tional feat which has been compared to a surgical incision and the grafting of a new organ into the body of the city.[38]

The site of No.78 South Hill Park is very different to that of the Maison de Verre. Although it was constrained by existing buildings, its immediate neigh-bours were modern. Along with these No.78 occupied a large incision into the fabric of the city, made not by the architect-surgeon but by Hitler and Goering's Luftwaffe.[39] It deliberately avoids any attempt to 'suture' the final segment of the wound that the site represented within this larger incision. Although No.78 South Hill Park was clearly designed to appear to be not only a 'machine for liv-ing in' but also a 'machine for perceiving the world outside' – specifically the much-prized view across Hampstead Heath and ponds – the form and structure of the house emphasise disjuncture, just as the views it allows of Heath and Ponds are fragmentary and collage-like. It adopts a different notion of architec-ture as a mechanism from which to view the world, an alternative Modernism that also has its roots in the 1920s and 1930s. In many ways the house is more like a Dadaist machine than a Modernist one. The perspectival, scopic views pro-duced by so many 'classic' Modernist buildings of the 1920s and 1930s – and those which 'reprised' Modernism in the 1950s – with their wide 'picture' win-dows can be seen as an extension of a world-view that is essentially a continua-tion of the Enlightenment project of the late eighteenth century. The 'controlling' viewing position assumed by the Modernist architects of the Howell, Killick, Par-tridge & Amis terrace houses was that of the (male) owner-occupier standing in front of his panoramic plate-glass window, gazing out across Hampstead Heath, in a manner not dissimilar to that of the eighteenth-century landowner.

By the 1940s and 1950s, large unmodulated areas of plate glass were em-ployed by Modernist architects to a degree beyond that used in the Modernist houses of the 1920s and 1930s (the most extreme examples were Mies van der Rohe's Farnsworth House and Philip Johnson's own house).[40] Although no-where near as – literally – spectacular as these, the Howell, Killick, Partridge & Amis terrace houses with their fully glazed end walls (and the modern penthouse extensions of the Victorian houses lower down the street) employ the transpar-ent and reflective qualities of glass to dramatic effect, both in terms of the view from their interiors and the view into these offered to a passer-by on the Heath.

However, such a use of glass is not unproblematic, whether in terms of gen-der relations or of politics. The plight of Edith Farnsworth as a single woman living in what amounted to Modernist greenhouse or conservatory is well docu-mented.[41] Very different to this, the Howell & Amis block, erected on the site of what had been a Victorian terrace destroyed by a German land-mine, confidently displays a rational and optimist faith in an enlightenment humanism, a belief that the forces of light had convincingly triumphed over those of darkness. As the Frankfurt school theorist Ernst Bloch wrote after the Second World War:

"The wide window, full of the outside world, requires an outside world that is full of attractive strangers, not full of Nazis. A glass door, stretching down to floor level, really does presuppose that, if there is going to be anything peeping in, or pouring in, it will be the sunshine and not the Gestapo."[42]

The world view projected by the Howell, Killick, Partridge & Amis terrace is one that seems to affirm an outside world of attractive strangers and sunshine ready to pour in, a world where the Gestapo have been convincingly vanquished.

In the 1940s and 1950s the notion of 'transparency' as a symbol of democratic values was retrospectively identified by Modernist critics with the glass and white-walled Modern Movement architecture of the 1920s and 1930s. However, in practice, an ideological association with glass as a material had not been con-

36. At about the same time a motorway was planned to cut across the East Heath to South End Green, though this would not have come so near to No.78. A public campaign prevented this from being built (Jean Stone, 'What nearly happened to South End Green', in SEGA: *the first 30 years*, London: The South End Green Association, 1996, p.5ff).

37. The tape recording of this interview remains unpublished.

38. See Frampton, 1966, *op. cit.* Le Corbusier often used the analogy of the Modernist architect as a surgeon cutting out the old diseased organs of the city to replace this with clean hygienic glass and concrete modern buildings. The architect and theorist Sarah Wigglesworth has recently argued that the way in which the Maison de Verre was inserted into the surgically invaded body of old Paris – like an in vitro fertilised ovum – is paradigmatic of the Modernist project. 'Maison de Verre: sections through an in-vitro conception', *The Journal of Architecture*, vol.3, Autumn 1998, pp.268–286.

39. The Victorian houses which previously occupied the sites of Nos 76–90 South Hill Park were destroyed by a land-mine which fell on the far side of No.1 Pond. The German bomber's target was presumably the nearby North London Line, a vital rail link between the factories of the North and Midlands, and London.

40. Among pre-war Modernist houses, perhaps only Mies' 1930s Tugendhat House in Brno compared, with its use of large areas of unmodulated plate glass.

41. Alice T. Friedman, 'Domestic Differences: Edith Farnsworth, Mies van der Rohe, and the Gendered Body', in Christopher Reed (ed.), *Not at Home: the Suppression of Domesticity in Modern Art and Architecture*, London, 1996, pp.179–192; Alice T. Friedman, *Women and the Making of the Modern House: A Social and Architectural History*, New York, 1998, Chapter 4, 'People Who Live in Glass Houses: Edith Farnsworth, Ludwig Mies van der Rohe, and Philip Johnson', pp.126–159. The Johnson House, on the other hand, represents a rather different kind of 'queerspace' to that discussed by Ofield (see Ofield, 1998, *op. cit.*).

42. Ernst Bloch, *Das Prinzip Hoffnung*, Frankfurt, 1973, vol.2, p.859, Translated in Ernst Bloch, *The Principle of Hope*, vol.2, Cambridge, Mass., 1995, p.734.

43. The exhibition was "intended to be the first annual presentation of German work" under the Nazis (Matilda McQuaid, 'Lilly Reich and the Art of Exhibition Design', in Matilda McQuaid, with an essay by Magdalena Droste, *Lilly Reich, Designer and Architect*, exhibition catalogue, New York: Museum of Modern Art, 1996, p.35). Reich remained in Germany during the war, though Mies left for the USA in 1938.

44. Since they moved into No.78 South Hill Park in 1964, the house has continued to be lived in by Brian and Margaret Housden with their children and later their grandchildren.

45. With reinforced concrete floors lined with white and blue Japanese earth mosaic, concrete and glass lens panel exterior walls, three-inch hollow cinder block exterior walls with a five-inch cavity, and interior partition walls, the bedrooms remained warm even in the bitter winters of the 1960s.

46. Housden says that the House was "built out of income" rather than capital, which was partly the reason why it has taken so long to complete.

47. These consist of one large rectangular and two small square sinks.

48. Frampton, 1966, *op. cit.*, p.261.

fined to the advocates of social democracy. Mussolini described Fascism as 'a house of glass into which all can look'. The Italian Rationalist architect Giuseppe Terragni designed the Casa del Fascio (Fascist Headquarters) in Como as an elegant transparent box that was intended to give built form to Mussolini's ideology of transparency and surveillance. Mies van der Rohe and his long-term collaborator Lilly Reich designed stunning displays of glass and transparency for an early Nazi exhibition 'German Work – German People' held in Berlin in 1934.[43] If the Modernist architects of the 1940s and 1950s – like the Modernist critics of the period – projected the use of large areas of glass as the material metaphor of the transparent and democratic welfare state, No.78 South Hill Park is a provocative questioning of such identification. The symbolism of its massive reinforced frame can perhaps be compared with the 'bunker archaeology' of the Hayward Gallery and Queen Elizabeth Hall and with other quasi-defensive structures of the 1960s, although it is unusual, perhaps unique in a domestic building of the period. In this context, the turn taken by Housden's design at the end of the 1950s and the beginning of the 1960s could perhaps be represented as an early example of the workings of a Postmodernist sensibility. This might be defined in terms of a questioning of the social ideology of received Modernism and an understanding of the plural and divergent (rather than the unitary and monolithic) nature of early-twentieth-century Modernism and an ability to draw both constructively and critically on this.

Nevertheless, the house also remains a very particular model of an idea of modern living – and of the role that the perception and experience of space and light (and the continuity and interaction between these) plays in this – which retains its sense of 'difference' and 'divergence' with a fresh directness after 35 years of continuous family occupation.[44] The impression given by the street facade with its unexplained sudden voids and jutting canopies of reinforced concrete is that of a building still in construction, of which the final form is not yet achieved. Although the house might appear superficially to be a rather rigid and fixed structure, it is in fact remarkably adaptable and has been able to incorporate many changes to its interior which has evolved gradually over 35 years of occupation. Some of these seem to have been envisaged in the original design. Other fixtures or finishes were deliberately not finalised in advance because, Housden claims, it was foreseen that future technical developments might make available new materials and techniques, as sometimes proved to be the case, while certain fittings or equipment were changed in line with technological or economic developments. The original central heating system installed in 1965 had an oil-fired boiler which was converted to gas in the 1980s, with under-floor water pipes serving the living and dining area on the lowest floor of the house and a hot-air heating system to boost this. Hot-water radiators were only installed in the two upper floors in the 1990s. The bedrooms remained without central heating for the first 30 years of occupation.[45] However this seems to have been largely due to financial constraints.[46] In many ways, the planning of the house was ahead of its time in its provision of creature comforts. Three of the four bedrooms were provided with ensuite facilities from the start, with individual toilets, washbasins and shower, while the fourth was equipped with a bath and washbasin.

A full-width balcony, cantilevered from the rear of the house at entrance level, was included in the original plans, overlooking the Pond and Heath. The concrete beams forming the supports for this were built when the reinforced concrete frame was cast, but remained skeleton structures for 35 years, before being completed with wooden decking. (The black-painted steel protective handrail and its supports were added in 1995, at the time when the gates at the front of the house were erected.) However, the horizontal concrete beams designed to support the deck of the balcony have effectively served for over 30 years as a pergola or *brise-soleil* for the patio area at the back of the house, which is directly accessible from the living/dining area.

As in many of the 'classic' Modernist houses of the 1920s and 1930s, much of the 'equipment at No.78 South Hill Park was deliberately selected and positioned to emphasise its technological aspects and to display the sculptural and symbolic qualities of heating and other modern domestic technologies. The large diameter cylindrical flue (originally installed to vent the oil-fired boiler) provides a strong vertical element rising through the living/eating area. This is painted in the same bright orange-vermilion as the exterior and interior metal surfaces of the Crittall windows. This colour was chosen for its suggestion of industrial red lead, and many of the fixtures are industrial standard fitments, like the MK steel light switches and thirteen-amp sockets and the laboratory sinks built into the island kitchen unit.[47] The pipes in the house are not enclosed but run prominently through the interior spaces, suggesting an organic as much as a technological symbolism. This may partly derive from the ways in which Chareau and Bijvoet organised the services inside the Maison de Verre.[48] But there are earlier precedents, for example in the house that Rading designed for the Weissenhofsiedlung model housing exhibition at Stuttgart in 1927, where the electrical wiring and the gas, water and heating pipes were exposed and colour coded,[49] "in a positively ornamental fashion", as a contemporary critic observed, standing out "like varicose veins".[50] As in Rading's Weissenhof house and the Maison de Verre, the technology of No.78 South Hill Park is exposed less as a metaphor of Utopian rationalisation than as a metonym for the human body and as a form of mechanical 'organic' ornament. The boiler flue and the forest of piping that rises from the basement boiler at No.78 dominates the dining space like a mechanical symbol of digestion and circulation.

In the planning of the house with its open areas and enclosures of space for different activities and occupants, Housden was influenced by the planning of the Maison de Verre and the Rietveld Schröder House, and by the way in which Van Eyck designed different areas of his Orphanage for different age groups of children. The changes of level and the manner in which windows and panels of glass lenses are used to admit (or obscure) light are also reminiscent of the ideas and practices of Adolf Loos.[51] In a famous passage about the Rietveld Schröder House, the Russian artist and designer El Lissitzky described the internal layout and arrangement of built-in furniture in the house as resembling the placement of houses in a city. With reference to the planning of both Van Eyck's Orphanage and No.78 Housden cites Palladio's idea (of which Lissitzky was probably aware) that "as the City is but one great House, or Family; so every Family, or Private House, is a little City".[52]

In its early years of occupation No.78 South Hill Park had less interior embellishment than it has subsequently acquired, although the carefully shuttered interior concrete surfaces and the circle motif inscribed into the concrete ceilings of the dining area, the master bedroom, the study area, and the concrete end wall of the garage area or car port could be considered as decorative or symbolic features. As in many Modernist houses, 'ornament' was largely provided by means of furniture. After visiting the Schröder House, the Housdens acquired fourteen pieces of original Rietveld furniture made by Rietveld's cabinetmaker and former assistant Gerard van de Groenekan.[53] Among these was one of the very few examples of the 1919 Buffet, which has served as a working sideboard in the dining area of No.78 since 1966. Many of the other Rietveld pieces have been in regular daily use for over 30 years,[54] as also have a set of Eames DKK-2 dining chairs (1953) purchased in 1967. Otherwise the original furnishings of the house were simple and minimal. Bedframes of block-plastered brick and wood were built into the bedrooms, but not cupboards and closets. Instead, each bedroom was provided with standard John Lewis, zipped, plain canvas wardrobes. These have been retained (or renewed where necessary) over the years.

The original fitments and finishes in No.78 South Hill Park were rather stark

49. Rading lived and practised in London from 1950 until his death in 1957. There was, however, no contact between him and Housden.

50. Edgar Wedepohl, *Wasmuths Monatshefte für Baukunst*, August 1927, p.399, quoted in English translation in Karin Kirsch, *The Weissenhofsiedlung: Experimental Housing for the Deutscher Werkbund, 1927*, New York: Rizzoli, 1989, p.162. Wedepohl noted that Rading had mounted the writing on small pieces of wood that projected some four or five centimetres or so from the walls, adding ironically that this "certainly does not make the house any simpler to keep clean".

51. Le Corbusier wrote in *Urbanisme* that: "Loos told me one day, 'A cultivated man does not look out of the window; his window is a ground glass; it is there only to let the light in, not let the gaze pass through'". (Le Corbusier, *Urbanisme*, Paris, 1925, translated in Beatriz Colomina, *Privacy and Publicity: Modern Architecture as Mass Media*, Cambridge, Mass., and London: MIT Press, 1994, p.234).

52. *The Architecture of A. Palladio*, translated by James Leoni, London: Printed by John Darby for the author, Second Edition, 1721, Book 1, Chapter XII, p.721. Housden argues that where Van Eyck joined together a number of 'family' houses to make a small urban community, he tried to make each part of the house like an individual house within a greater whole.

53. Cf. Brian Housden, '"Jolly Nice Furniture": A Note on the Work of Gerrit Thomas Rietveld', in *2D/3D: Art and Craft Made and Designed for the Twentieth Century*, exhibition catalogue, Sunderland Ceolfrith Press, 1987, pp.54–56.

54. As well as the Buffet, Rietveld gave the Housdens a Red Blue Chair, a wengé wood version of the High Back Chair, a Berlin Chair, End Table, Piano Stool, Child's Wheelbarrow, Military Chair, Military Stool, Military Chair with Arms, Zig-Zag Chair, Zig-Zag Chair with Arms, Zig-Zag Table and a white-painted Crate Chair. These were shown in the De Stijl exhibition, at the Camden Arts Centre in 1968, and in the South Bank Centre exhibition, *Rietveld Furniture and the Schröder House*, which toured Britain and Ireland in 1990–91.

and plain, whereas recent additions to the interior have been executed in more luxurious materials. In the mid-1980s Housden bought a number of industrial woodworking machines which he temporarily installed in No.78. He took a City and Guilds course in wood machining at the London College of Furniture which enabled him to complete some of the interior fixtures and fittings himself. In the early 1990s the cast concrete stairwalls were capped with balustrades of book-matched Norwegian black, white, pink and green marble.[55] The dimensions for one piece of capping – in a prominent position at the top of the flight of stairs leading down to the living/dining area – were apparently mis-measured by the fabricators. Housden says he believes in incorporating such mistakes and, rather than having the capping recut, used three offcuts of marble to make a pedestal

figure 5
The rear elevation and garden to the house.

for a small sculpture.[56] The dining table was designed in 1994. Housden constructed the heavy teak frame himself. The huge circular top is made from two semicircular book-matched leaves of polished black slate (carboniferous limestone), embedded with large fossil oyster and scallop shells, from a quarry in Leighinbridge, County Carlow in the Republic of Ireland.

These later embellishments and furnishings are reminiscent of Adolf Loos's interiors where fine woods and book-matched marble facings are used as decorative elements, i.e. 'real' or 'natural' materials rather than ornamental representations of nature. The association displayed here between the 'natural' and the 'synthetic' (or between 'nature' and 'culture') is closely linked to the way in which the 'cladding' of the exterior of the house – to use Loos's 'Semperian' term – both refuses and affirms, through its 'skin' of glass lens and concrete panels, an intimate and yet 'distanced' relationship between the inhabitants (or visitors) and the 'natural worlds' of the Heath and Ponds beyond.

55. Made by Dispecker Ltd.
56. By Stephen Cohn, Wells Coates's son-in-law.

2 Architecture and the Landscape Obligation

PETER ALDINGTON

figure 1
The Miller House, Frank Lloyd Wright.
The house grows out of the garden – it is
impossible to tell where one begins and
the other ends.

Architecture and the Landscape Obligation

PETER ALDINGTON

RECENTLY a landscape architect friend started enthusing about a part-time teaching job he is doing in a school of architecture. He explained that the (final-year) students were part of a 'Landscape Option' – in other words they opt to pay particular attention to landscape as part of their on-going design projects. But, I said, "isn't there an obligation – not an option – for all of us, students or not, to consider the landscape, whether it's a rural or an urban one, in everything we design? Isn't it impossible to design any form of construction, either above, below or over the ground without it affecting that ground and its immediate environs?" "Yes," my friend replied, "but at least it's a start and I'm able to get at some students before their ideas about landscape become too fixed and we find dialogue impossible, because your profession and mine speak different languages". What a damning indictment of the schism which has grown between our two professions.

This encounter reawakened an old hobbyhorse of mine about the inevitability of involving the landscape every time we design anything. In the days of my frequent visits to schools of architecture, as either visiting critic or external examiner, I was constantly amazed to find that the only consideration students gave to the environment of their designs was that of the paper they were drawn on. They frequently told me that they had lectures about landscape, but that these seemed to have little relevance to their design work. It rarely occurred to them that we inevitably affect the environment when we build, and that at the very least we have an obligation to respect it. Neither did they seem to be taught that today's technology provides us with opportunities to use external space in ways which could not have been dreamt of before the twentieth century.

Prior to the advent of twentieth-century technology, building designers were constrained by the necessity to build massive external walls to support and create enclosure. In other words they had little choice but to build boxes, and create openings in them for light and passage. Even with this huge constraint many of them realised the importance of the landscape in creating a suitable setting to enhance the enjoyment of their buildings.

But today, no such constraint exists. We have total freedom to add or remove walls as we please. Walls can be opaque, transparent or translucent, massive and heavy or lightweight and delicate, fixed or moveable. But what do most of us do with this unexploited freedom? We build stylised boxes, we chop holes in them for windows and doors, and we all too frequently ignore what goes on outside the box.

The early Modern Masters didn't do this. They saw twentieth-century technology as the great liberator from the constraint of the enclosing wall, and they started to unify interior and exterior space. The barriers between inside and outside had been lifted and architecture was able to embrace a whole new dimension. The pioneers of Modern architecture had great visions that living with nature might be made possible by technology:

figure 2
The Barcelona Pavilion, Mies van der Rohe, 1929. Still a supreme example and a poetic vision of what might have been. Never before and rarely since has the maxim that 'less is more' been so beautifully realised. No plants, but landscape none the less. (Photo of reconstruction of original building)

"The room must be seen as architecture, or we have non architecture. We have no longer an outside and an inside as two separate things. Now the outside may come inside and the inside may and does go outside. They are of each other. Form and function thus become one in design and execution if the nature of materials and method and purpose are all in unison."

"This dawning sense of the Within as reality when it is clearly seen as Nature will by way of glass make the garden be the building as much as the building will be the garden: the sky as treasured a feature of daily indoor life as the ground itself."

"You may see that walls are vanishing. The cave for human dwelling purposes is at last disappearing."

"Walls themselves because of glass will become windows and windows as we used to know them as holes in walls will be seen no more."

The Natural House, Frank Lloyd Wright, 1954

Or:

"... the introduction of the completely free standing wall in Mies van der Rohe's 1923 project for a Brick Country House... In this work the walls were treated as clearly defined individual load bearing entities, placed in a semi-overlapping manner in order that any one area of the house was not rigidly enclosed, but rather subtly defined in its relationship with other areas. By this decellularisation, the space flowed freely as a continuum throughout the house, and since walls were often pulled out beyond the roof plane into the landscape, the defining line between interior and exterior was minimised. This liberation of interior space was developed further in 1929 at the Barcelona Pavilion."

Mies van der Rohe at Work, Peter Carter, 1972

figure 3
Barnstaple House. This early photograph shows the different building 'edges' defined by the various elements. (Photo Richard Einzig)

Now, more than 50 years on, it is clear that we have failed to exploit our ability to integrate exterior and interior space. We have ignored much of what the early Modern architects were telling us, preferring instead to see Modernism as a superficial style, rather than understanding the philosophy which led to the creation of the forms. We are still producing boxes and ignoring the external spaces or, at best, treating them as optional extras. In failing to develop and build on the ideas and ideals of this pioneering generation we have lost over half a century. There are very few houses or buildings of any kind which better these early examples of internal and external spatial integration. We have the technology to perform wonders, and the best of our architecture uses technology in exciting and creative ways, but when it comes to thinking about the spaces round and between our buildings we are frequently to be found wanting. Why? Could it possibly have something to do with education? If landscape is an 'option' in our schools of architecture, an option which attracts only a small percentage of the total design mark, then what hope is there for an understanding of the design potential of outside space?

The ideas, ideals and examples of the modern pioneers provided much of the inspiration for the work of my own practice. Perhaps the nearest we came to an

integration of inside and outside spaces was in a small house designed in the early 1970s just outside Barnstaple in North Devon. The fairly complex spaces sit under a simple double-pitched roof, supported by three rows of timber posts. This means that none of the walls is load bearing and they do not have to reach the roof for reasons other than privacy. Our clients were used to large high-ceilinged rooms, and they were loath to lose the spaciousness these provided; yet they also wanted a small house to retire into. By using a frame and a tent-like roof, we were able to make a living room with a small footprint into an apparently endless space. More than half of the 200 sq metre roof is visible from the twenty sq metre living area and the visual space continues out into the valley. The cut in the valley side which contains the house continues out at living area level, and is partially enclosed on two sides by grass banks, the third side being the valley view. The tiled floor reaches out into this space with no level change and minimum visual interruption. The roof over-sails part of the external floor, but its supporting posts are back from the edge. The sliding glass wall is on another line and the curtains are another still. So there is no one definable 'edge' to this corner of the house and our clients were able to achieve their desire both to live 'in' the valley and to have a small yet spacious house.

Very early experiments with breaking down the inside-outside barriers were made at a house in Prestwood, Buckinghamshire. Here we defined two categories of space – those which required privacy or semi privacy, and those which could be more 'open' and possibly less well defined. The private spaces are enclosed by brick 'boxes', some becoming towers and reaching up through two floors, where they have a stabilising function for the timber-framed first floor.

figure 4 a,b & c
Barnstaple House [a & b] "The tiled floor reaches out ... with no level change and minimal visual interruption. The roof over-sails part of the external floor, but its supporting posts are back from the edge. The sliding glass wall is on another line and the curtains another sill". [c] "A small footprint into an apparently endless space".
(Photos Peter Aldington)

The more open spaces weave between and are loosely defined by the 'boxes', but are not enclosed by them in any formal sense. These spaces are also 'transitional' between the fully or partially enclosed 'private' areas and the outside. Sliding glass walls open onto a water garden, partly covered by the overhanging first floor, which acts as another transition between inside and outside, leading the eye from one to the other and inviting a journey across its stepping stones.

Building design and garden design are both about manipulating space. The skills needed to design covered spaces (buildings) and uncovered spaces (gardens) are the same. In our designs we have tried to create a continuum: the building doesn't stop at its enclosing wall and the garden doesn't necessarily start there either. The inside and outside spaces are equal components of the living environment, and often the two are inextricably intertwined.

figure 5
Prestwood House. Stepping stones 'inviting a journey'. (Photo Richard Einzig)

figure 6
Prestwood House. The water garden acts as a transition. (Photo Richard Einzig)

My beliefs about architecture and design have developed over the years taken to design and make three houses and a garden at Haddenham. To understand these it is important to know something about the place. Haddenham is a village of strong and individual character. Its houses are, in the main, built out of 'wychert', which is made from the local clay puddled with straw. This material and the way it has to be used (how it 'speaks' to those who use it) determine the character of the village. The village literally 'grew' out of the earth it stands on, and it feels like that too. There are miles of walls – not hedges, but walls, defining boundaries, providing enclosure and creating privacy. These walls are rendered, have stone bases and tiled tops to prevent damp rising and rain soaking.

The houses were to be built in the middle of a village born out of the needs and ways of life of a very different age, a village grown gradually over many centuries, with buildings of all ages telling their own stories. The buildings we were

figure 7
Askett Green. My first village house, a
box which contains the structure.
(Photo Richard Einzig)

going to add to this tapestry had to tell their own story also, but it must be today's
story, not yesterday's negotiated with adding icing sugar. Yet their story must
also be firmly based on the stories told by the other buildings, a continuation of
a living tradition.

The site is between two village streets, Townside and High Street, and has its
own strong character, providing many constraints which have helped shape the
design. There is a group of tall trees on the east boundary, emphasising a bend
in the High Street. We are the guardians of this important feature in the village.
A large horse chestnut and two walnuts in the centre, a group of acacias on the
southern boundary, a wychert wall dividing an old orchard from a vegetable garden and a cottage at the south-west corner flanking the only entry point, all had
a determining role to play in considering the building layouts. The aim was to
create here an environment of today for today's car-borne commuter/business
man who lives a fast and stressful life and whose house, I felt, should be a spir-
itual haven away from that world, and yet clearly grown out of it.

As well as being a response to what I felt and saw in Haddenham the design
is a reaction to, and development of, the work done and lessons (some subconscious) learned from the first house I had built, three years earlier, Askett Green.
There, a structure-based aesthetic had been developed, and this was further re-
fined at Haddenham; but the principal change is that at Haddenham the buildings are made to 'embrace' outside spaces by not building a 'box' which contains
the structure, but allowing the structure to speak outside, and using it to define
external spaces which use the same materials as the internal ones.

The masonry 'box' has been disintegrated, windows are no longer 'holes in
walls' to let light in, but gaps between walls which are closed with folding glazed
doors or large areas of glass. There are still some tiny holes punched through the
walls, but these are to provide lighting interest or views at specific places as a
contrast rather than a main theme. The material chosen for the masonry elements is a foamed concrete block, which creates a bold scale but is not weather
resistant, needing the protection of external render to protect it from rain and
frost erosion, just as the native material of Haddenham does.

The houses open into and embrace outdoor living spaces, which are extensions of the interior spaces. Living areas face south and west into these courts,
but receive high-level east light from the other side, even when this is 'borrowed'
from the neighbouring garden. Bedrooms which face north, away from the out-

door living spaces, look over gardens from a slightly raised floor level. Living areas and bedrooms are linked by the third element, circulation/dining/kitchen, with the kitchen area in the centre of the house creating a focus for all its activities yet visually and spiritually a part of the outside.

The largest of the walnut trees is in the geometric centre of the site, and this became one of the strongest influences on the eventual layout. The houses, which wrap round a private 'public' court, join in an echelon shape on their east sides. So the east wall is always a boundary, except at Turn End, our own house, where it forms a wall to the garden. There is a view right through from the entrance in the west to this east wall, which has been pierced with a glazed door leading out into a contrasting world ... a spring woodland garden. The eye fo-

figure 8
Turn End. The houses define a public/private court. (Photo Richard Bryant)

figure 9
Turn End. The kitchen/dining/circulation space looking into the outside living space or court. (Photo Richard Bryant)

figure 10
Turn End. Inside and outside living spaces flow smoothly together. Notice the continuous floor tiling. (Photo Richard Bryant)

cuses on a large urn by Monica Young placed on the axis of this east/west route. This pot is central to the whole design: it draws you through the house and into the garden, and once you are there it provides a reference point back to the house.

A woodland path leads from the garden door to a grass 'glade' which curves diagonally across the site to create the longest vista possible. This element is used to tie together all the other garden elements or 'rooms'. The urn is also at a focal point of the view down the glade, as well as terminating a subsidiary grass walk. None of these visual axes is reflected in the ground plan. They are just there as sight lines, and provide a structure to what otherwise might easily become an amorphous collection of spaces.

Other more formal areas have developed as the garden was enlarged, and the designs for these have reacted to and grown out of the buildings and spaces around them. New axes have been set up by making openings through walls or building pergolas or piercing buildings, but they all lead eventually back to the initial glade, or 'ribbon', which ties the whole composition together. Trees have been carefully added to reinforce the axes and to take over when the inevitable happens and the apple trees die or fall over.

The central walnut tree still stands, clearly demonstrating its pivotal role in the whole layout. The group of acacias became the generator for Turn End's court. There is now only one of these, as about fifteen years later they became too large to be realistic in such a small space. The pond is the result of a direct decision to move a young walnut from here to its present site in the entrance.

I believe that the structure of a design, whether it involves buildings and interior spaces or gardens and exterior spaces, should be powerful enough to allow furnishing or planting to be flamboyant, or even apparently out of control, without masking the basic structure. So whether planting is doing a job, like enclosing, screening or emphasising, or is disciplined in colour, shape or texture, it can be allowed to 'happen'. Over the years we have added rugs, pictures and the inevitable trivia of a lifetime to the interior, plants have been added to the garden in their hundreds, even the birds and the bees (and the judicious use of home-made compost!) have made some wonderful contributions, but the designs have been strong enough to accept these changes.

I have used these examples to try to demonstrate something of the thinking of myself and my former practice. I have concentrated on just one small aspect of that thinking. It would be too simplistic to assume that the exploitation of interior space was our only concern in the complex business of creating architecture; in the same way that it is wrong – and dangerous – for students to be led to believe that landscape is an 'option'. There is an obligation for all architects

figure 11
Turn End. The west/east vista through the house and onto the garden to the urn. (Photo Richard Bryant)

figure 12
Turn End. The east wall is pierced to reveal the woodland garden beyond. (Photo Richard Bryant)

figure 13
Turn End. The east wall of Turn End from the spring woodland garden. (Photo Richard Bryant)

to concern themselves with exterior spaces and the immediate environs of buildings. This just may be beginning to happen, for I sense a new awakening of interest in the landscape and its relation to architecture. Maybe all is not lost; but we architects need to get off our backsides – we have over half a century to make up!

The garden at Turn End is open three times a year for the National Gardens Scheme. The house and garden are usually open once a year around mid summer. The photographs of Turn End illustrating this article are from a set of colour pictures taken by Richard Bryant during the past three years for a book, *A Garden and Three Houses*, written by Jane Brown, published by Garden Art Press. The Landmark Trust is in the process of acquiring the house near Barnstaple, which is one of the projects featured in the Landmark Appeal, launched in May 2000. For further information contact the Trust on 01628 825920.

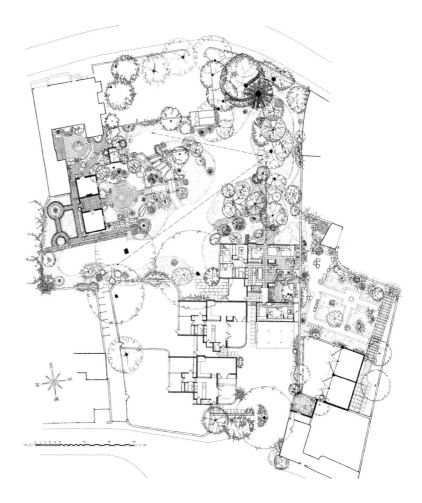

figure 14
Turn End. The diagonal grass glade also focuses on the urn.
(Photo Richard Bryant)

figure 15
Turn End. Holes in the walls have been made and other axes set up, the house from the formal gravel garden to the south. (Photo Richard Bryant)

figure 16
Turn End. An axis created through an existing garden building.
(Photo Richard Bryant)

figure 17
Plan of the houses at Haddenham and Turn End garden showing principal visual axes. Other more formally structured axes are not marked.
(Plan by Ronald Wilson)

3 The houses of Patrick Gwynne

NEIL BINGHAM

The houses of Patrick Gwynne

NEIL BINGHAM

TODAY, Patrick Gwynne still lives in The Homewood, near Esher, Surrey, the house he designed for his parents in the late 1930s.[1] The Homewood was more than just a spectacular beginning to Gwynne's architectural practice. Because he has lived there for most of his life, and has been able to make changes and additions, Gwynne has obviously developed a close relationship with the house. Sir Denys Lasdun, a friend of Gwynne's from their young days together in Wells Coates's office, calls The Homewood "the great love of Patrick's life". Created during the early years of Modernism, the house developed and flourished with the architect's style, becoming an experimental showcase, where the architect has been extraordinarily creative in his designs for furniture and fittings, the use of materials, the ordering of the architectural and garden space.[2]

Gwynne was only 24 years old when, in 1937, he began to design The Homewood.[3] He had just left the office of Wells Coates, where he had worked at the very cutting-edge of the Modern Movement. Although undoubtedly The Homewood was created under the influence of Le Corbusier's Villa Savoye, the bedroom wing bears a striking resemblance to Shipwrights, a small house near Hadleigh, Essex on which Gwynne had worked in Coates's office; and the marble fireplace and wooden wall in the living room owe a debt to Mies van der Rohe's Tugendhat House. But for all its influences, The Homewood is distinctive in its own right. It is a sizeable country villa with two wings, lying at right angles to one another. The longer wing contains the bedrooms for family and guests; the T-shaped wing comprises the living rooms, service areas and staff quarters. Joining the wings is a block, or as Gwynne often refers to it, "a bridge", with a spiral staircase. Most

1. Born in 1913, Gwynne now leads a retiring life, though he is still very active completing a commission for an extension to 2 South Parade, Chiswick, London, and replanning his ten-acre garden. Often he is consulted about his built works – usually by former clients and new owners. Gwynne has made provision to leave The Homewood to the National Trust, which has gratefully received his offer.

2. It became the place where he tested ideas; many elements at The Homewood are repeated in the more than a dozen one-off houses Patrick Gwynne designed between 1949 and 1985. It can be difficult to distinguish whether a unique piece of design was used first at The Homewood. Indeed, Gwynne emphasises that he has not "consciously" used ideas from The Homewood. Yet time and again one has to return to the architect's own house for the source or exemplar.

3. The Homewood has been featured most extensively in *Architectural Review*, vol.88, Sept 1939, pp.103–16 and *Country Life*, vol.187, 22 July 1993, pp.84–87.

figure 1 (opposite page)
Grovewood, Sunningdale, Berkshire.

figure 2
The Homewood, Esher, Surrey, the living room (photographed in 1939) and plan.

of the living spaces are on the first floor – giving views across the garden; structurally the upper level is raised on brick piers and concrete piloti.

Two major features of the house are its strong geometric proportioning and its flexibility. Gwynne applied a modular of 4ft horizontal to a 1ft 8ins vertical; almost all the elements, from window sizes to ceiling heights, are a variation on this ("We were always getting out our set-squares," he jokes). The living spaces are large, open and flooded with natural light; the original furniture was lightweight, easy to push aside for dancing on the sprung maple floor. This tension between the apparent rigidity of the building proportion and the relaxed atmosphere of living is characteristic both of most of Gwynne's houses, and of Gwynne

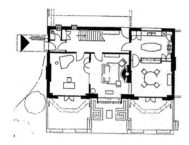

figure 3
115 Blackheath Park, London. Exterior and plan.

himself, an elegant gentleman, disciplined in his lifestyle and business practice, yet humorous and ever ready to find a witty solution to a design problem.

Patrick Gwynne returned to architectural practice after serving in the RAF during the Second World War. Restricted by the government's measures, which naturally favoured public housing and reconstruction over private development, Gwynne began working on small jobs, mainly for bombed-out houses and shops.[4] One was of significant scale and importance. The Victorian house at 115 Blackheath Park, in Blackheath, southeast London, owned by Leslie Bilsby, had suffered severe bombing. Gwynne had met Bilsby in the mid-1930s, when he had

4. However, he did land the large commission for the Crescent Restaurant in the Festival Gardens, at the 1951 Festival of Britain. This brightly coloured, large, semicircular tented structure was engineered by Felix Samuely and the restaurant managed by Charles Forte, who was to become one of Patrick Gwynne's major clients.

accompanied Wells Coates to an exhibition of modern chairs at Whiteley's department store in Bayswater. Bilsby had helped organise the show, mounted startlingly by hanging the pieces on the wall. With his many connections in the furniture trade, Bilsby was engaged by Gwynne to act as the consultant for all the major cabinetwork at The Homewood. Bilsby eventually became Gwynne's principal client, commissioning numerous projects, many of which were not built.

Gwynne, in 1949, retained what remained of the structure of Bilsby's house, but radically altered both its internal and external appearance. Gwynne adopted, for the first time, a distinctive tripartite facade arrangement. Based upon the extant and very traditional composition of the Victorian house, with its central en-

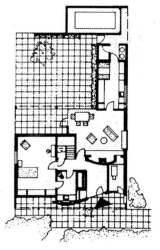

figure 4
Hawkins House, Bournemouth.
Exterior and plan.

trance flanked by windows at ground-floor level, Gwynne applied a rigorous geometry of three identical openings (by using standard steel window and door frames), giving access to the three square rooms behind. To emphasise and make the module unit expressive, canted wooden posts divided the elevation into three verticals, while serving to hold the deep roof overhang and upper-storey balconies. The surround of the front door was also canted.[5]

Another decade passed before Patrick Gwynne built his second principal house, in 1958, a full twenty years after The Homewood. The client was the film and television actor Jack Hawkins, who had commissioned a small house for his mother-in-law for a leafy but conventional street, at No.31 Glenferness Avenue, in Bournemouth. Once again, the architect used the tripartite facade, this time with a whimsical curved brick wall in the centre of the ground floor. Because the occupant was handicapped, accommodation was restricted mainly to the ground floor, although two bedrooms and a bathroom were set on the floor above. The roof was pitched, so as to not make the house stand out too much from its neighbours. Instead of a garden, the Hawkins house had a courtyard, which created a sunny and easily maintained enclosure, screened from nearby houses.

Almost concurrent with the Hawkins house was a major commission for a house in Hampstead, north London, completed in 1959. This was the first of three new-build houses Gwynne created in the area, which, coincidentally, were all for German émigrés – clients, it seemed, who proved receptive to the architect's Modern ideas and unusual design solutions. The Firs, for Otto and Marion Edler, was finely sited at the top of Spaniards End, a newly created cul-de-sac. The panoramic views to the south demanded that Gwynne orientate all the major rooms towards this outlook. As a result, the lesser rooms at the back were of minor size, creating a plan tapering to the rear.

5. Bilsby sold the house to Span, and the house was torn down and replaced in 1967 by a development of houses, Parkend, by Eric Lyons.

The tripartite facade of The Firs is reminiscent of the Bilsby house a decade earlier, with free-standing verticals, in this case metal poles, supporting the first-floor balcony the length of the first floor and the deep roof overhang. Where the curved wall appeared in the Hawkins House, with the Edler house an expansive, bowed, single-sheet glass window projects over a pool. The interior is rich, and for the first time since The Homewood, Gwynne could take advantage of a generous budget to create features such as panelled walls, fitted furniture, a polished Napoleon marble fireplace (modelled on the one at The Homewood) and, a few years later, a purpose-made settee with a built-in gramophone. One of the architect's many special effects included a boxed unit in the fireplace wall, which rotated the television to face into the sitting room, or to the other side into the dining room, or hid it when closed.

Gwynne's next house – Past Field, Rotherfield Road in Henley-on-Thames, Oxfordshire – was on a large site, so he abandoned the double-height tripartite arrangement in favour of an elongated, V-shaped, single-storey plan. The house was on the brow of a hill, so all principal rooms were placed towards the view south. The bend in the middle of the long house and the deep overhang imparts a sense of enclosure, and breaks what could have been a monotonous stretch. The plan also allowed for extensions at either end; the clients, a young physician and his wife, Dr and Mrs A.J. Salmon, asked Gwynne back six years after completion in 1960 to add the master bedroom at one end and a new dining room and kitchen at the other.

In the same year as Past Field, Patrick Gwynne undertook his only speculative development. The client was his friend Kenneth Monk, who acted as Gwynne's quantity surveyor on almost all of his projects. Monk lived in Kingston upon Thames, Surrey, and bought a house on Coombe Hill Road, which he found "unpleasing". He had it demolished and replaced by four houses by Gwynne. Instead of the usual strip sites off the main road, the communal driveway of the old house was retained and the houses grouped around a landscaped

figure 5
The Firs, Hampstead, London. Plan and exterior.

court. All the houses were similar: rectangular in plan, two storey, flat roofed and with staircases in the middle, lit by skylights. But each was constructed of a different colour brick. These four extremely elegant boxes were linked by garages and garden walls of serpentine shape, which the architect felt was "the key" to the overall unity, as well as a credit to Monk for providing features not considered "functionally" necessary.[6]

Patrick Gwynne's other two new-build Hampstead houses are on adjacent plots in the then recently developed cul-de-sac of Beechworth Close, off West

Heath Road, which had been created from the garden of a large older house. The Bruh House, 4 Beechworth Close, was finished in 1961, and occupies the most attractive section at the end, with beautiful mature maples and a large pool, surrounded by willows. Here Gwynne encountered the design problem of having to place the house facing down the garden, of northern aspect. His solution was to use a rectangular plan, with a part of the upper of the two stories slightly set back, and then to slice the corner of the living space with glazing, allowing for views and light. Southerly light was brought in through a large window at the opposite end of the space, which faces onto a partially covered patio and small inclined rock garden.

Mr and Mrs Max Bruh were good clients "from the aesthetic point of view," recalls Gwynne. They ran the successful fashion house of Frank Usher. The architect worked with them on the design of the garden, bringing in his own gardener. The interior was one of his finest, opulent in the architect's usually restrained manner. The staircase hall "was very much a feature," says Gwynne. Some walls were panelled, others shimmer in Italian glass mosaic – black under the stairs, bright orange in the kitchen – while the sitting and dining rooms are faced in plastic covering to simulate Japanese grass paper, a material which the architect used at The Homewood to replace the 1930s grass paper which had faded.

Having admired the Edler house, Mr and Mrs Hornung turned to Patrick Gwynne to design a house for them, on land formerly occupied by the tennis court of the large house. The property was not large, but it had a fine outlook on one side, across a wooded area of Hampstead Heath. The Hornung House at 3

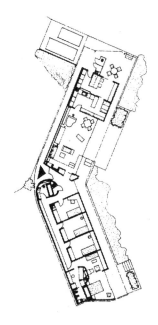

figure 6
Past Field, Henley-on-Thames. Exterior and plan.

6. Of the four Coombe houses, one has been drastically altered, and another destroyed.

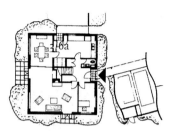

figure 7
Coombe Hill, Kingston upon Thames.
Exterior and plan.

figure 8
Bruh House, Hampstead, London.
Exterior and plan.

Beechworth Close, completed in 1963, was a sculptural version of Gwynne's speculative houses in Coombe Hill: similar in plan with a combined living-dining room, study and kitchen on the ground floor; bedrooms on the first floor; and a very fine central terrazzo staircase, the walls panelled and pierced with slotted inset shelves for ornaments (very much a Gwynne feature). The loose rectangular plan was shaped to a "tub-like form" by curving the corners and walls on either side of the front and rear entrances.[7]

While working on the later Hampstead houses, Patrick Gwynne had been engaged in the design and supervising the building of his largest house – Witley Park in Surrey. Slightly greater in size than The Homewood, Witley Park is, as Pevsner says, a "very lavish" country house. The client was Gerald Bentall, proprietor of the large department store bearing his name in Kingston upon Thames. When Bentall bought Witley Park, a farming property of more than 2,000 acres, the estate's great late-nineteenth-century house had been destroyed by fire, although the outbuildings remained and the famous underwater grotto with a billiard room, in the ornamental lake, survived. Gwynne would have preferred to have sited the new house overlooking this picturesque lake scene, but Bentall chose an open sloping field with nothing but a small spinney on one side, upon expansive flatland extending as far as the South Downs.

Because of the great size of the house, the brick construction of most of his previous dwellings seemed unsuitable, so Gwynne turned to tougher building methods of almost industrial standard. Like The Homewood, Witley Park is two stories high, with the ground floor of the house principally for service areas, a garage, covered terraces, a study and office; the upper floor is given over to a large living area, dining room, sun terrace, kitchen, bedrooms and staff flat. The house sits on concrete columns and walls, whose exterior has been covered with a warm Hornton stone. The top storey is constructed from a light steel structure, from which are hung, off steel hooks, exterior panels of pre-cast, aggregate-faced concrete panels. Large windows are placed at most of the corners to concentrate the distant views.

The architect designed many of the interior fittings at Witley Park, from the lighting fixtures to the built-in banquettes. Of particular beauty and ingenuity were the principal staircase and the living room fireplace wall. The staircase in the grand entrance hall is like a theatrical magic trick. Each terrazzo tread is independent, suspended in space by cantilevering from the wall on a steel tube; the suspended effect is heightened by hidden lights at each end, which illuminate the wood-panelled wall. The handrail hovers, without a single balustrade, its only support from the edge of the top landing; it is constructed of a steel RSJ section clad in shaped teak. Patrick Gwynne recalls that the heavy handrail "suited the client", who was "a bit dour".

The masterly crafted wall in the sitting room is similar to the fitted wall in The Homewood, with its internally lit insets, swing-round drinks cupboard and hideaway cupboards for television and slide projector. The arrangement of this fitted wall did not suit the later owners of Witley Park, Sir Raymond and Lady Brown, who asked Gwynne back to remove it and design a much simpler solution for housing their collection of books.

By the mid-1960s, Patrick Gwynne had begun to gain his first public commissions since his 1951 Crescent Restaurant. His most well known buildings of the period are the Serpentine Restaurant in Hyde Park, London (finished in two stages, 1964 and 1971, and now destroyed) and the large addition to the Theatre Royal, York, of 1967. In these and his other works, especially the Dell Restaurant in Hyde Park (1965) and the doctor's surgery in Henley-on-Thames (1970), Gwynne created plans and building shapes of an extremely organic form. The Serpentine, for example, was formed by clustering concrete pillars like giant mushrooms; and with its shallow copper dome suspended above glass walls, the Dell floats over the water's edge as if it were an oversize pond lily.

Patrick Gwynne's exploration of architectural planning had begun with The Homewood and now, in maturity, reached a sophisticated and innovative phase. In architecture and design generally, the 60s and 70s were a period of experimentation and stimulation, a relaxation of the order inherent in the war years. Though Gwynne's architecture never approached the radicalism of Archigram or the Smithsons, it remains self-disciplined, stylish and provocatively individual. Having started designing as part of the early Modern Movement, by rejecting historical style and embracing modern methods of construction, Gwynne now continued to push his design principles and passions to a degree which can still astonish.

No.10 Blackheath Park is "a design which sets out to shock", writes Pevsner.[8] Indeed, in this second house for Leslie Bilsby, the architect had a client who had always sought progressive Modernism. Bilsby had become a very successful property developer, with many of his enterprises centred in and around Blackheath. Since the mid-1950s, he acted as a director of Span, working in conjunction with the company's principal architect, Eric Lyons, in developing many of the more than nineteen modern housing estates built mainly in the gardens

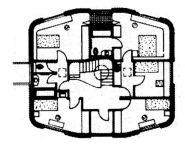

figure 9 (left)
Hornung House, Hampstead, London.
Exterior and plan.

figure 10 (right)
Witley Park, Surrey. Exterior and plan.

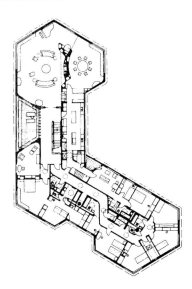

of Blackheath's large Regency houses. No.10 Blackheath Park, which was finished in 1969, stands between two such older houses, and although Gwynne followed the same roof lines, and poised the new house on a raised ground floor like its neighbours, the architect says that he "conceived this house with no pretence of joining up". Both the front and garden elevations are similar, strikingly dark and sleek, treated in black slate facings slashed by horizontal bronze-tinted glazing. The street entrance is sculptural, the front door approached by circling around a fountain in the centre of a semi-circular stair on one side and ramp on the other (created for Bilsby's mother, who was in a wheelchair), then across a metal drawbridge.

Because Leslie Bilsby enjoyed giving parties, he asked Gwynne not for large rooms but intimate areas where the guests could group yet feel part of the whole festivities. So every major living space (and consequently the bedrooms above)

7. A later owner destroyed the central staircase of the Hornung House and replaced it with one designed by Eva Jiricna.

8. The Buildings of England, *London 2: South*.

of No.10 Blackheath Park is the same size. And, giving a most fascinating impression, each room is a pentagon. At the rear, a metal staircase leads down into the immense and beautiful garden, designed by Ivor Cunningham, the principal landscape architect for Span. On the principal floor of the house there are small linking spaces with built-in metal and glass sideboards. Some of the walls are covered in Gwynne's favoured plastic grass paper, others in black plastic. The sliding screens between the living rooms, which make for even more private spaces, are lacquered a bright red.

Having been left a widower, in 1979 Leslie Bilsby moved from the five-sided rooms of No.10, to the eight-sided spaces of No.22 Park Gate, also in Blackheath,

figure 11
Witley Park, entrance hall.

figure 12
10 Blackheath Park, London.
Exterior and plan.

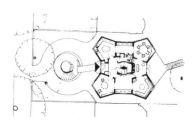

designed by Gwynne to be "a real bachelor pad". This brick house, which turns its back on the road to look instead down the disappearing vista of the long garden, is arranged as three linked octagons. The largest has at its centre a fireplace, around which were grouped areas for sitting, eating, cooking and study. One of the smaller octagons contained the master bedroom; the other the garage with two small guest rooms above.

Gwynne had suggested a similar house for Bilsby as far back as 1960, when the developer had attempted, but failed, to purchase another site in Blackheath.

This had been a house planned as three overlapping circles. But No.22 Park Gate more ingeniously had links between the blocks, which could be used for a laundry, workshops, storerooms and the passage to the garden. The house's form also recalled the two motorway service buildings at Burtonwood, Cheshire, on the M62, which Patrick Gwynne had designed in the early 1970s – these too were octagonal, with sloping roofs. Bilsby had said he "wanted a house rather like a tent". Gwynne's solution evoked memories of his 1951 Crescent Restaurant for the Festival of Britain. The next occupants of No.22, Colin & Jacqui Hawkins, invited Gwynne to make changes to the house to better suit family living. The architect moved the kitchen out of the main octagon to the service area, which

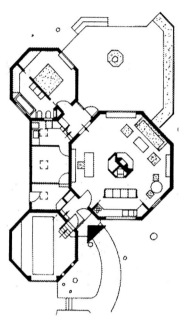

figure 13
22 Park Gate, London.
Interior and plan.

he felt was a much better arrangement than the original, and repositioned the master bedroom up to a new storey.

In 1965, just prior to the Bilsby house in Blackheath Park, Patrick Gwynne had designed another unusually planned house – Grovewood, West Drive on the Wentworth Estate, in Sunningdale, Berkshire, for Mr and Mrs David Shaw. On a beautifully wooded site (to which Gwynne added banks of ferns, heather and rhododendron) Gwynne created a house shaped like a propeller – three splayed wings pivoting on a hexagonal core. The upper floor was of white vertical boarding, floating over the lightly recessed ground floor of dark brick. As at Past Field, the clients anticipated adding an extra bedroom at a later date, which was eventually constructed over the garage. Sadly, a later owner demolished the house.

The architect's quantity surveyor, Ken Monk, asked Gwynne to design him a summerhouse at Angmering on Sea, West Sussex, on a strip of land overlooking the Channel. Although Angmering has its fair share of seaside architectural horrors, it can also boast a handful of outstanding houses from the 1930s, including Runnymede, by Gwynne's mentor Wells Coates (completed with Pleydell-Bouverie), and the internationally celebrated Sea Lane House by F.R.S. Yorke and Marcel Breuer. The Monk House, on Tamarisk Way, completed in 1970, was designed to avoid looking at the neighbours but instead take full advantage of the sea view. There are not, therefore, many windows on the side walls. The house is planned with an hourglass shape, narrowing to a "waistline" for the staircase core. The roof echoes the undulating walls, sliding from the

figure 14
Plan, Grovewood, Sunningdale,
Berkshire.

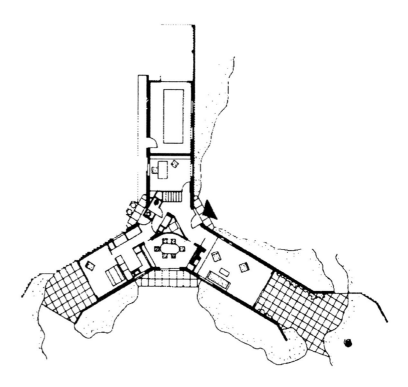

front to the rear like a giant wave. Gwynne chose building materials, many of them man-made, to withstand the harsh sea-front climate: plastic fascias and garden screens, steel windows finished in black acrylic coating and balustrades and handrails with nylon coatings.

Perhaps Patrick Gwynne's most organically shaped house was Amanda, Meadway, near Esher, completed in 1971, whose plan the architect refers to as a "wasted circle". The clients, Mr and Mrs Knowles, had purchased a long plot of land near The Homewood, adjacent to Esher Common. Lying close to the houses on either side, Gwynne wrapped the specially made, curved brick of the sinuous walls of the new house in such a way as to give directed views. Even the windows were "blinkered", with wide frames that tilt away from the offending neighbours. The garden side of the house is scooped out beneath a wide overhanging roof. An exterior balcony on the first floor is reached by a spiral staircase, a feature that the architect enjoys because, like at The Homewood, the host can greet visitors from the balcony and then together they can enter the house directly into the principal rooms.

Another job done for close friends was a major conversion in 1971 of a large Edwardian house at 3 Kidderpore Avenue, Hampstead, for the Hollywood film actor Lawrence Harvey and his wife, one of the most famous models of the period, Paulene Stone. Gwynne had designed a house ten years earlier for Harvey, on a site in Windlesham, Surrey. But that project had been abandoned when Harvey received a filming contract and moved to California. Gwynne went out to visit Harvey and admired the three excellent houses which the actor had commissioned by American architects at Malibu, Beverley Hills and Palm Springs.[9] In converting the Hampstead house, Gwynne tried to create a residence "that might have been in Beverly Hills."

The "rather useless features" of the old house, like the bay windows, were removed, the attic converted for the children and maids, the living room ex-

9. Patrick Gwynne even designed a Malibu Beach house, which was not built, for Lawrence Harvey in 1972.

10. Lawrence Harvey also bought modern furniture, including the classic leather Eames lounge chair and ottoman. When Harvey died, his widow gave this set to Gwynne – "nice to have to sit on, as well as a nice memory," he says.

tended to create a sun lounge, and a new wing added for garage, sauna and studio. The entrance door was "Larry's demand", which pleased the architect, for a design the actor had used on one of his California houses: a tall slit with a geometric patterning of square panelling. The interior was another of Patrick Gwynne's well-appointed exercises in built-in fitments for audio, storage and shelving, many with special lighting effects. One of Lawrence Harvey's sidelines in America had been dealing in antiques, so his own impressive collection of furniture and objects enriched Gwynne's setting.[10]

In winter, when the trees in the garden of The Homewood are without their leaves, it is possible for Patrick Gwynne to glimpse, in the distance on the hill to the south west, the last house he designed. The exterior of the crescent-shaped Winterdown, dating from 1984–85, is another of the architect's strong statements in contrasting light and darkness; in this case the warm mustard colour of the brick against the darkness of the windows and the semi-glazed black roof

figure 15
Monk House, Angmering-on-Sea, West Sussex. Exterior and plan.

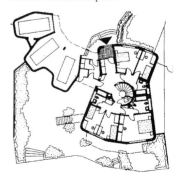

tiles. The brick was carried through to the principal living spaces of the interior, which is open-plan in accordance with the client's wishes. The client, Robin Fawcett, a dealer in cultured pearls and expert in Oriental customs, was an experienced Japanese cook, so special cooking arrangements were made in the centre of the kitchen.

While working on these private house commissions, Gwynne continued to make alterations to his own house. The most apparent addition to the exterior of The Homewood was the enamel mural by the artist Stefan Knapp, who was also responsible for the enamelled splashback behind the serving area of the dining room. And, using the sparkling colours of Murano glass wall tiles, which he

figure 16
Amanda, Esher, Surrey.
Exterior and plan.

favoured in many of his kitchen designs, Gwynne created an abstract panel at the garden entrance which intertwines a plan of the house with his name and the name of the house. Internally there were very few structural changes other than the enlargement of one of the bedrooms. The master bedroom was converted into Gwynne's architectural office, and part of the staff quarters to fitness rooms as an adjunct to the new outside pool. The kitchen was redesigned in the early 1970s, with surfaces covered in the architect's favoured plastic cloth and a central, boat-shaped tiled working table placed in the centre, a feature which Gwynne had used in many of his kitchen designs as far back as 115 Blackheath Park in the late 1940s.

The lightweight furniture in the living and dining rooms was replaced by more permanent items, mostly designed by Gwynne. These elegant pieces often

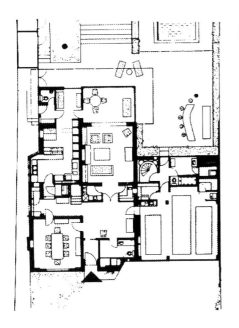

ingeniously incorporate other functions: the sofa has a hidden projection screen which slides up from the back; the white laminate writing desk converts to a drawing table; and the long reading table has drop slots and a splicing machine for editing home films. The round dining room table is very playful, with its circular well sunk in the middle which can either hold flowers or be used to uplight an object covering it. A row of knobs at the host's fingertips controls brightness and allows a choice of three coloured lights.

Patrick Gwynne's original clients, and those individuals that today live in the houses he designed, always speak enthusiastically of these homes. There is almost a sense of wonderment as they run their hands over the plastic wall-coverings and describe the on-going amusement of opening wardrobe doors and having the light pop on automatically. With great respect, clients relate how Gwynne keenly worked out the details and then assiduously maintained a high level of skilled execution from his craftsmen.

Having designed and built for more than 60 years, Patrick Gwynne has been practising architecture through almost the whole period of Modern Movement in Britain. His style is unique, yet his houses nevertheless respond to historical developments and inspirations: from the 1930s functionalism of early Modernism based on Continental examples, to the immediate post-war rationalism of

figure 17
3 Kidderpore Avenue, Hampstead, London.

figure 18 (below left and above)
Winterdown, Esher, Surrey. Exterior and plan.

figure 19 (below)
The Homewood, Esher, Surrey (photographed in 1999).

the Case Study houses in California, to the organic expressionism of such architects as Frank Lloyd Wright. But Gwynne always added a personal and very English touch to all his designs; so that, although today it is fashionable to abuse the thesis made popular by Pevsner that the Modern Movement in England grew out of its strong historical past, Patrick Gwynne's knowledge and use of materials and his love of novelty may be interpreted as an Arts and Crafts inheritance. In much the same way, the convincing integration of his houses and their gardens is an echo of this country's great landscape tradition. In other words, the houses of Patrick Gwynne have maintained the consistency of the best in British domestic architecture.

I would like to thank Patrick Gwynne for his patient assistance with this article. Between 12 October 1997 and 6 February 1999, Patrick and I recorded six 90-minute interviews on his life and career. These are deposited with the National Life Story Collection, National Sound Archive, British Library, 96 Euston Road, London NW1 2DB. Words and phrases quoted in the text are from these interviews. Also, my thanks to Luis Peral for helping to digitise the house plans, which were drawn by Patrick Gwynne. Many clients and present owners of Mr Gwynne's houses have been generous and hospitable, including Lady Brown, Mrs Anne Bruh, Colin & Jacqui Hawkins, Dr and Mrs A.J. Salmon, William Sargent & Sharon Reed, the late David Shaw, Peter & Susan Taylor and Leslie Bilsby's daughter, Tanya House.

Conservation, restoration
and addition: Work at Long Wall,
Long Melford, Suffolk

HUGH PILKINGTON

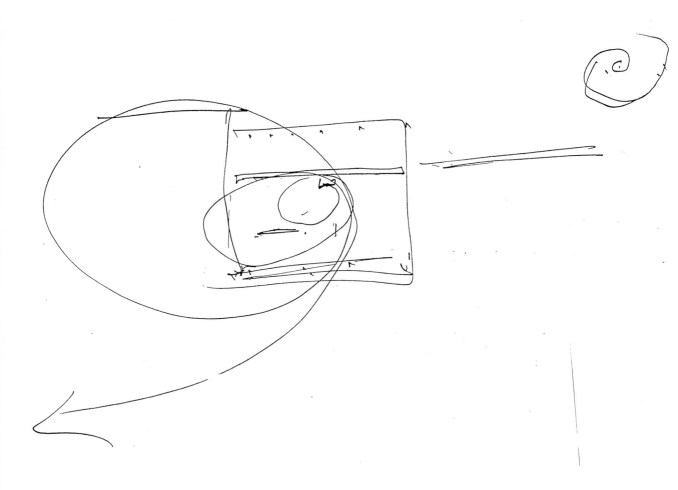

figure 1
A sketch by Philip Dowson of Long
Wall, when it was completed.

Conservation, restoration and addition:
Work at Long Wall, Long Melford, Suffolk

HUGH PILKINGTON RIBA

"This small house is of considerable importance, and one of the few built in England since the war which stands comparison with the best foreign examples"[1]

LONG WALL was commissioned by Mr and Mrs E.V. Williams in 1962 from Sir Philip Dowson, their neighbour at Pembroke Studios in London, after the couple had found somewhere which, Sherban Cantacuzino points out in his review of the house in 1965, "was a site on which planning permission had been granted long before present day restrictions in rural areas were imposed".[2] The house was to be a weekend home, then a permanent home when the Williams retired: "it had to be easy to run, quick to heat and future maintenance kept to a minimum."[3] Money was to be spent on "square feet rather than finishes and fittings. The cost was not to exceed £5,000".[4] Dowson was then working at Arup Associates, and he worked on the design with his assistant at Arups, Peter Foggo. The house is credited to Dowson and not to Arup Associates. The concept of the house appears to be Dowson's, the detailing Foggo's. Max Fordham, then a young friend of Dowson's, advised on the novel heating system used in the house.

I first saw the house in autumn 1994, when it was advertised for sale in the *Architects' Journal*. Mr Williams had died, and Mrs Williams was no longer able to live in the house alone. I had a client who was looking for a contemporary house, or a site on which to build one, so I alerted them to the sale and went to see it with them. I approached Sir Philip Dowson and suggested the client contact him to hear more about the house. The purchase, however, did not proceed – the client is still looking for a site! But nearly a year later Sir Philip contacted us to say that the eventual purchasers, Mr and Mrs John Burke, had contacted him about extending the house, and that he had suggested they employ me.

The couple needed another double bedroom, with a new bathroom and a utility room. But they also wanted the existing bathroom and kitchen to be upgraded and the whole fabric of the house refurbished. I was aware of the considerable

1. Sherban Cantacuzino, *Modern Houses*, 1964, Dutton/Vista.
2. Sherban Cantacuzino, *Country Life*, February 1965.
3. Ibid.
4. Ibid.
5. Ibid.
6. Society for the Protection of Ancient Buildings, *The purpose of the SPAB*, undated leaflet.
7. Ibid.
8. Department of National Heritage, *Listing Schedule* TL845E-992/8/1009.

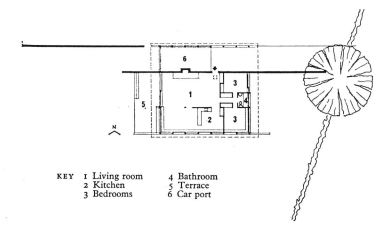

figure 2
Plan of Long Wall (From Sherban Cantacuzino, *Modern Houses*, 1964, Dutton / Vista).

KEY
1 Living room
2 Kitchen
3 Bedrooms
4 Bathroom
5 Terrace
6 Car port

importance of the house. The works proposed, if undertaken within the fabric of the existing house, did not require planning permission, only building control approval. I investigated the possibility of spot listing so the client could take advantage of VAT relief on alterations, and alerted both the Babergh District Council Conservation Officer and the Regional Inspector of English Heritage to my proposals. Both endorsed my approach.

For the new works, we proposed converting the open car port/workroom into the bedroom and bathroom. We formed a closed entrance area, with access to the utility 'cupboard'. This remedied one of Cantacuzino's original criticisms,[5] and levelled the entrance approach, remedying another. In undertaking these works, I used only joinery details employed in the original house. The new bathroom was, however, entirely contemporary. The existing bathroom was completely removed and matched details in the new one. The kitchen was remade and extended using current equipment. Some of the cupboards were retained and repaired. Others were made up to match the originals exactly.

The restoration of the original house was another matter. I spoke again to Sir Philip Dowson about his original intentions. I wanted to know if there was anything he hadn't been able to do due to the tight financial constraints when the house was first built. The only detail he would have changed, it seemed, was the wide windowsill, which was of linoleum – he would have liked tiles, "like the bar at Snape Maltings". He also did not like some of the work the Williams had done to the house subsequently – the addition of a solid fuel stove and flue and chimney, and other shelving that "defaced the purity of the whole". We were later able to remove these and make the windowsill detail as Dowson had originally intended.

For my approach, I used the SPAB guidelines over issues of conservation, repair and restoration. The SPAB maintains that buildings should be mended with a minimum loss of fabric.[6] Loss of fabric means the removal of "romance and authenticity". If restoration is the "return of old buildings to a perfect state" it can lead to the "unnecessary renewal of worn features and the hypothetical reconstruction of missing elements".[7] I prefer this SPAB approach of "skilful repair" – "new work expressing modern needs in a modern language", in turn relating "new to old in a way which is positive and responsive".[8] I thus felt it appropriate that new work was undertaken using existing details, unsightly later items being removed. New work used matching materials where these were still available. Externally we remade the roof fascia, as the original timber was now rotten. These were machined to match the original mouldings. We uncovered the original coping detail. The original aluminium coping was refurbished and reused.

One of the greatest problems in the conservation of twentieth-century buildings is the architect's love of new and novel materials. We all in our current practice like to use newly advertised and promoted materials, elements and

figure 3
Long Wall before work began
a) General exterior of the house
b & c) Note the poor condition of the
wall and the ragged landscaping
d) Interior, kitchen diner.

techniques. We all want to make silk purses with sows' ears – using cheap materials carefully to make expensive or stylish elements. These are often difficult to match and replace when they either fail or wear out. They often don't perform well in use if not carefully (and often expensively) maintained.

The external garden walls had subsided and cracked. New bricks had to be stitched in. We had difficulty in obtaining imperial Flettons. We wanted to double-glaze the glass infills in the converted carport with sealed units, but we could not match the original obscured glass so placed secondary glazing internally instead, thus avoiding moving the original glass and causing possible irreplaceable damage.

The building was designed for, and built of, inexpensive materials. But these are no longer inexpensive, nor are they easily available. American and Canadian conservation measures have had an impact on the price and availability of western red cedar. European timber was used in repairs. The panels used to face the internal walls were shuttering ply, though the quality of present-day shuttering ply has been seriously reduced and it is no longer faced with roll-cut veneers – strip veneering is now the preferred facing veneer. We found supplies of high-grade boarding that came close to the original look. We had to replace some of the parquet flooring where it had been removed and where we were making up floor levels, and managed to find a local source of imperial parquet that matched the original. The internal varnish had also deteriorated considerably, but we carefully matched the tone of the original fabric on new work to maintain the 'overallness' of the building. External stains were of 'Architectural Solignium', no longer available in the original specification. Azko Nobel provided a matching specification for the material and application after some extensive trials on site.

The heating system, designed by Max Fordham, works like a car heater. A fan blows air over heating elements, so that heating is virtually instantaneous. The intake/output used a clever device of fin blades using cut-up Venetian blind slats. Venetian blind slats are now thinner and metric, but we did manage to get new ones that make a close match to the originals, which had been irretrievably damaged. The system still works as intended after an extensive overhaul.

In working on Long Wall we came across interesting theoretical considerations. The building as built was not the building as conceived. The infills on the carport/workshop wall were originally specified as "corrugated asbestos sheeting". Obscured glass in a small diamond pattern was eventually used. The walls were to be "concrete block walls plastered internally", but, in the end, were built of Fletton bricks, not concrete blocks. If built of materials originally conceived by Foggo, the building would have appeared considerably harsher and more brutal. As it is, it is softer, finer and romantic – more Dowson.

The external walls as drawn are plain flat elements. One garden wall had to

be rebuilt as it was blown over soon after being built. It was rebuilt with reinforcing reveals rather than as a straight element. Another garden wall has buttresses to reinforce it. The Flettons were painted white externally, though there is no indication if the concrete blocks were to have been painted externally.

Dowson explains the theory behind the building in terms of Greek altars and temples in a landscape, the raised platform and regular columns suggesting this. The plan "spirals out from the core of the building, the hearth, into wider uses within the building and eventually out into the landscape". The way that the walls extend into the garden is similar to the design for a Brick Country House (1923) by Mies van der Rohe and his Barcelona Pavilion (1929). Others have pointed to Frank Lloyd Wright when considering the roof overhangs.

figure 4 a, b & c
Long Wall after work.

When work was completed the building was listed Grade II. Sir Philip visited the building and was delighted at the result. The original surviving commissioning client, Mrs Williams, described the work as beautiful – wishing she could have done it. The new owners Mr and Mrs Burke were pleased with the result and with Sir Philip and Mrs Williams' reaction. They appreciate and enjoy the custody of an important building, and the result eventually mitigated the annoyance of the time overruns on the contract due to difficulties in obtaining suitable materials. Long Wall has thus, with the integration of equipment to current standards, been given life (with considerate maintenance) for another hundred years.

5 Against the grain: the domestic architecture of Robert Harvey

LOUISE CAMPBELL

figure 1
The architect's own house, Ilmington,
1957, living room.

Against the grain: the domestic architecture of Robert Harvey

LOUISE CAMPBELL

WARWICKSHIRE ("Shakespeare's county", as the signs at the county boundaries style it) is more generally associated with timber-framed buildings, picturesque towns and rolling countryside than with inventive modern houses.[1] But between 1954 and 1979, Robert Harvey, a Stratford-based architect, designed over 30 houses which serve to challenge assumptions about how it might be appropriate to build in such surroundings, and how a clientele, which comprised businessmen, village schoolteachers and professional people, might choose to live. They also suggest the existence of what might be called an alternative strand in British Modernism, something of a different and more robust character from that which is usually emphasised in accounts of post-war architecture.

Writing about the sources of his own architectural inspiration, Peter Womersley distinguished between what he called 'heart' architects like Frank Lloyd Wright, with their intensely personal approach to, and involvement with, their buildings, and 'head' architects like Mies van der Rohe, with their overtly rational and disciplined approach. It is often assumed that the 'head' architects dominated the British architectural scene.[2] This does not in fact appear to be the case. Wright's Fallingwater of 1937 evidently made an overwhelming impression on Womersley.[3] He was not alone. Lionel Brett compared the atmosphere in May 1939, at the packed Henry Jarvis Hall of the RIBA, where Wright delivered his lectures on 'Organic Architecture', to that of a revivalist meeting. "The great man expected to address a learned society, only to find himself mobbed by an army of future conscripts...We were carried away," recalled Brett.[4] The British fascination with Wright lasted through the post-war period. Wright's work had a double appeal: his Usonian houses demonstrated to architects in the 1940s – as they had to architects in the 1930s[5] – that it was possible to design a Modern house with limited means, while other projects demonstrated a rich and emotionally satisfying language of architecture which struck a responsive chord.[6] Scottish architects like Basil Spence, Robert Matthew, and the partnership of James Morris and Robert Steedman seem to have been particularly susceptible to his influence, responding to post-war restrictions on building, and to shortages of materials and labour, with house designs which ostentatiously hugged the earth and made reference to vernacular building traditions.[7] But Wright's impact on a later generation of architectural students declined significantly in the later 1950s. In 1959, the year of his death, the annual RIBA conference took for its theme the social function of the architect. Richard MacCormac points out that the contrast between the image of Wright as individual creator and that of the architect as servant of the state, then current in Britain, could scarcely have been greater.[8] Many architects who entered practice during this decade eschewed Wright's romanticism in favour of greater restraint and clarity. For this generation, his influence was rapidly overlaid (although never quite effaced) by that of Mies.

Robert Harvey was born in Coventry in 1919 and studied architecture at the Birmingham School of Art. He remembers finding the lectures on town planning

1. In the foreword to the Warwickshire volume of The Buildings of England, Pevsner and Wedgwood wrote in 1966: "Regarding private houses [of the twentieth century], none need a reference in this Introduction" (p.48). Ironically, Harvey's South Winds and Womersley's Cedar Leys were completed the previous year.

2. T. Dannatt, Modern Architecture in England (1959) and A. Jackson, The Politics of Architecture (1970) both stress the legacy of Mies.

3. P. Womersley 'Architects' Approach to architecture', RIBA Journal May 1969, p.192: "In my teens I saw photographs of the Kaufmann house, Fallingwater, and this decided me on my career. I still think this is the most beautiful house ever built..."

4. 'Work and Theories of Frank Lloyd Wright: II – Influence in this Country', Listener, 12 December 1946, p.838. For a useful summary and analysis of contacts between Wright and Britain see D.L. Johnson, Frank Lloyd Wright versus America: the 1930s (1990).

5. James Dunnett has identified the influence of Wright in Goldfinger's Broxted house of 1936–7. 'Roots of Goldfinger's design', Architects' Journal, 28 March 1996, p.24.

6. Brett, p.839. "Elegance of construction and richness of texture are just what we want at the moment, if only to drown our sorrows in ... Wright's organic architecture reaches us just as we have abandoned social formality, just as we are feeling heartily sick of austerity."

7. Spence recalled that he considered going to work for Wright in 1950. D. Pryce-Jones, 'Pillar of Architecture', Sunday Telegraph Magazine, 28 September 1973. For a discussion of Wrightian influences see M. Glendenning, R. MacInnes and A. MacKechnie, A History of Scottish Architecture from the Renaissance to the present day (1996), pp.440–1 and 455–6. For Morris and Steedman's 'Avisfield' of 1955 see C. McKean, Edinburgh: an illustrated architectural guide (1992), p.162.

8. Paper on 'Frank Lloyd Wright', 'The Special Relationship' conference at the Architectural Association, London, 30 October 1998.

9. For example, Harry Gibberd (b.1914), who entered Birmingham Architects' Department in 1954, or Douglas Chalk and Bill Pearson who joined Coventry Architects' Department in the mid-1950s.

10. See A. Powers, *In the line of Development: F.R.S. Yorke, E. Rosenberg and C.S. Mardall to YRM 1930–1992* (1992), pp.9–10.

11. Womersley, *op. cit.*, p.194.

12. It is unclear what this publication was. There was considerable coverage of Wright (although few illustrations) in British journals during this period. Wright's 'An Organic Architecture' appeared in serial form in the *Architects' Journal* ('Recollections: United States 1893–1920' between 16 July and 6 August 1936; his 'What the cause of architecture needs most' in *Architectural Review* in March 1937. An exhibition of photographs of Wright's buildings was held at the Building Centre during his visit to London in May 1939, when the Architecture Club, the MARS group and the AA also entertained him. For reactions to his lectures, see especially the editorial 'Frank Lloyd Wright', *Architects' Journal* 11 May 1939, RIBA Journal 22 May 1939, p.700 and Wright's reply in RIBA Journal 16 October 1939, p.1005. A special Wright edition of *Architectural Forum* was published in the US in January 1938.

13. "You propose a great honour. I accept, gratified that during this terrific war England can think of honouring an architect. A culture like that can never lose." RIBA Journal 13 January 1941, p.37.

14. On 14 July. His speech is printed in *Architects' Journal* 27 July 1950, pp.86–7.

which he attended at the university dull, and the ones at the art school more interesting. At first glance, the Birmingham School could seem to have functioned as a seed-bed for the development of a modern architecture in Britain: Frederick Gibberd and F.R.S. Yorke emerged from the School in 1929 and were active as writers and propagandists for the Modern Movement, as well as founding important private practices. Many others went to staff the growing city architects' departments in Coventry, Birmingham, Bedfordshire and elsewhere after the war.[9] But perhaps the School spawned other kinds of things too. George Drysdale, trained at the Ecole des Beaux-Arts, was apparently less doctrinaire as a teacher than A.E. Richardson. In the inter-war period, a residual concern with the Arts and Crafts seems to have lingered in the School, managing to coexist with the new kind of architectural education.[10] In looking at the history of British architecture from about 1930 and 1960, we have come to consider as the norm a pattern in which architectural training on site gave way to formalised architectural education, and in which the traditional emphasis on independent practice was eclipsed by a growing interest in social architecture. But Harvey does not fit into this pattern. Although finding the classical tradition stultifying, he disliked the Modernism of architects like Le Corbusier almost as much. He showed very little interest in working in the public sector. Nor, apparently, did he wish to diversify his practice in line with the expanded opportunities offered by the post-war period.

Harvey also differs from his better-known contemporaries in that domestic architecture does not constitute his early work or a sideline, but was a major part of his practice over a period of twenty years. Womersley lucidly spelled out the reasons why an ambitious architect entering practice during the 1950s might elect to abandon this kind of work: "Modern house design … entails extraordinary involvement with a personal client; it falls foul of planning officers and building societies; and the demands made upon a practice as far as time, drawings and supervision are concerned, are still totally incommensurate with the financial return."[11] Yet these demands seem to be precisely the sort of things which Harvey relished. The delight in shaping environments to suit the idiosyncrasies of individual clients and the contours of the particular site are as evident in his work as they are in that of an architect like Philip Webb. But, at the same time, the fascination with a new language of architecture, and the desire to create new kinds of interior spaces and a soothing environment in which to retreat from the combat of modern life, mark out his architecture as belonging to the booming industrial heartland of England at mid-century.

Harvey recalls the shock of being shown an article about Frank Lloyd Wright in a magazine in the late 1930s.[12] He was particularly struck by photographs of Midway Gardens, where, due to the fact that it was an entertainment complex, Wright had been able to create freely and expressively. In 1940, having completed four years at the School of Art, Harvey joined the army. Classed as unfit for active service because of a limp, he was able to spend time writing his thesis on Malvern farmhouse buildings and reading. Harvey acquired copies of Wright's *An Organic Architecture: the Architecture of Democracy* (the Sulgrave Manor lectures given at the RIBA in 1939), and first editions of Henry-Russell Hitchcock's *In the Nature of Materials* (1942) and Wright's updated *Autobiography* (1943, originally published 1932). A letter he sent to Taliesin requesting information about Wright's recent work elicited a graceful response. Echoing the cable sent to the RIBA accepting the Royal Gold Medal for 1941,[13] Wright wrote to the young architect that he was touched to hear that there was interest in his work in beleaguered wartime Britain.

After the war, Harvey went to work for J.B. Cooper, from whose office he was given a day off to go to London in July 1950 in order to hear Wright speak at the annual prize-giving at the Architectural Association.[14] At about this time, Harvey joined the office of Leonard Harper, father of his contemporary and friend Ross

Harper, in Birmingham. Harvey and Ross Harper together submitted a remarkable design in the Coventry Cathedral competition, its ground plan based on a series of hexagons and the seating arranged in a fan shape around the altar.[15] It was to Leonard Harper that the elderly F.W.B. Yorke, Stratford-based architect and father of F.R.S. Yorke, came to ask for assistance. By 1951, the two firms had amalgamated, with Ross Harper and Yorke running the Birmingham office, and Harvey given charge of the Stratford one, where he inherited what he calls "a load of trouble" – houses begun by Yorke. At the same time, it represented Harvey's big chance. Starting in 1954, Harvey began to specialise in the design of private houses in the Stratford area. Other regular clients were the National Farmers' Union Insurance Company, for whom Harvey designed new offices,[16] King Edward VI School in Stratford, Flower's Brewery, for whom they modernised many pubs and designed three new ones,[17] the Midland Bank, and the Royal Shakespeare Theatre, for whom he designed new dressing-rooms and the Riverside Restaurant. Through his connection with the theatre, Harvey was able to ask the joinery workshop during the off-season to make fittings for some of his houses.[18] In 1961 his wife Bet, who had also trained at Birmingham, joined the office. She describes her role in the practice as that of an "enabler" rather than a designer; she suggests that her contribution was to survey sites, to write specifications, and to produce drawings.

Harvey's first house (and the only one to feature in a national architectural periodical) was designed in 1954 for a site outside Tanworth-in-Arden. A low-slung brick house with a compact L-shaped plan, it represents what was in many ways an ideal of family life in the 1950s. In the open-plan living area, spatial excitement was generated by extensive use of glass and a living room whose ceiling rose into the roof-space; the internal angle of the plan was used to create a sheltered terrace. A sense of intimacy and enclosure was created by varying the ceiling heights where appropriate, by cladding them with birch plywood panels, and by the use of deep eaves, which framed the view from the range of wide, south-facing windows and provided protection against glare. Harvey described his approach to the design in terms which are strongly reminiscent of Wright: "It was thought of from inside, bearing in mind its relation to the site, and after a list of required accommodation had been given by the client."[19]

Two small houses designed for relatives in a woodland setting between Kenilworth and Coventry followed in 1956–7. That for Harvey's brother resembles the Tanworth house in the arrangement of its accommodation; however, it

15. Illustrated in *Architects' Journal* 30 August 1951, p.262.

16. In Scholars' Lane, Stratford, where he altered the street front of the NFU building, and at Tiddington, where he extended a building designed by Yorke in the 1920s. See *Truscon Review* no.25 (c.1959), p.4.

17. The Yard of Ale in Birmingham Road, Stratford, The Rose (now called The Lockhurst Tavern) in Lockford Lane, Coventry of 1964 and The Lord Lambourne in Peterborough.

18. For example the magnificent mahogany joinery at Tall Trees, Tredington in 1963.

19. 'House for Mr. K.B.L. Bailey at Tanworth-in-Arden', *Architect & Building News*, 13 November 1957, p.631. A selection of houses by Harvey is discussed and illustrated in F. Mark and C. Cronin, 'Warwickshire's hidden houses', RIBA *West Midlands Yearbook* 1983, pp.69–78.

figure 2
House for Harvey's brother, Kenilworth Road, Coventry, 1957, bedroom wing.

is far more romantic in the way in which it nestles into its setting and more mannered in its detailing. It presents the visitor with an inscrutable brick facade, pierced by narrow, high-set windows, and by the deeply shadowed recesses of the entrance porch and carport, flanked by a massive brick pier. The diamond shape and the hexagon are a recurrent motif in the design. The bedroom wing is terminated by angled end walls and enlivened by elaborate brickwork under the eaves. The ceiling of this room (a bedroom designed for three small boys) is of cedar and mahogany, and designed rather like the roof of a wagon, with a shelf running around the whole room at high level, and built-in beds, dressing table and desks. The living-dining room also has a boarded ceiling with diamond-

figure 3
House at Frog Lane, Ilmington, 1959, exterior.

figure 4
House at Frog Lane, Ilmington, 1959, sitting room.

shaped roof lights and a low timber cornice containing recessed light fittings. Viewed from the rear, the space of the house appears to form a continuum with that of the garden thanks to pivoting doors, a raised terrace, shallow brick steps and a brick flower box. Disliking down pipes, and reluctant to spoil the dominant horizontals of his design, Harvey here devised an ingenious alternative, in which metal chains acted as a channel for rainwater to run off the cedar shingled roof to the ground. He was to use this feature in many subsequent houses. Here too begins an enduring concern to integrate shelter for the motorcar within the envelope of the dwelling.

Around 1957, Harvey, having fought (and won) a long battle for permission to build a house for himself in Chipping Campden, and then discovered that his intended site had been sold, purchased an area of orchard above the south Warwickshire village of Ilmington. Built of Cotswold stone, English oak, and with floor surfaces laid with polished slabs of greenish-brown Hornton stone from Stanley's quarry near Banbury, the house combines to a remarkable degree an interest in the inherent qualities of building materials with a sophisticated understanding and manipulation of space. The house is organised around a massive chimney stack which forms the focal point of the living-room; from this core, the house spirals outwards, its windows designed to take advantage of extensive views over the north-eastern escarpment of the Cotswolds.

After the foundations were laid and work on the house had begun, costs apparently threatened to get out of hand and Harvey himself took over much of the building work, helped by his brother and brother-in-law, both of whom were accomplished joiners. He specified that the stonemasons should not break the stone up into chunks, but should instead produce long pieces, which he laid himself in courses with a pronouncedly horizontal emphasis. This rather mannered approach to the stonework resembles that in Wright's Taliesin East and the Miller house of 1952. In Harvey's house we find an unexpected synthesis of the Arts and Crafts tradition of sound building using local materials with an entirely Modern sensibility. Between the late 1930s and 1950s, architects like F.R.S.

Yorke, Leslie Martin and Denis Clarke-Hall had also experimented with the visual contrast between well-laid stone walls and lighter-weight materials.[20] Harvey's close engagement with his materials and the surrounding terrain, although superficially comparable, suggests something altogether more elemental and subjective. Harvey has defined his architecture as "a three-dimensional sculptural thing", and describes his approach as more akin to that of a builder or a sculptor, concerned primarily with the particular qualities of his materials, rather than with aesthetics *per se*. For him, aesthetic considerations, although important, must follow on behind.[21]

A series of houses designed by Harvey for clients in Ilmington, between 1958 and 1965, reveal a sensitive response to different sites, clients and budgets. The earliest, built in Frog Lane for an elderly client and his wife, was built of Cotswold stone with a cedar-shingled roof. The roof (which in this house had to cover first-floor rooms) was calculated at a pitch which reconciled the house, located near the bottom of the valley, with the steep incline of the surrounding land. The underside of the generous projecting eaves was painted white in such a way as to reflect light into the interior. The drawing room and dining room had dropped ceilings around their perimeter; painted a pale colour, these intensified the natural lighting of the interior and accommodated elegant recessed light-fittings set into elegant glazed boxes. The combination of this low perimeter with a raised area at the centre of each room creates a sense of spaciousness and ease together with a pleasant sense of containment. Framed by the dark-stained woodwork of the windows, views over the garden and the village are given additional horizontal emphasis by the broad timber-edging strip around the raised portions of the ceiling.

20. See Powers, *op. cit.*

21. Interview with Robert Harvey, April 1997. Compare Wright: "Is the idea that good architecture must be first of all, good building and the architect a master-builder first and an aesthetician afterward – heresy?" RIBA *Journal* 16 October 1939, p.1005.

The next, for the village schoolteacher, was a delightful house designed to a circular plan, and built in 1962 on a sloping site. A bank at the rear of the house was retained, and the house sunk into it. The focal point of the single living room is a pot-bellied stone fireplace, whose form recalls that of an old-fashioned bread oven. The house, with its tiny kitchen, two little bedrooms and bathroom, contains an array of ingenious devices to maximise space and minimise clutter: sliding doors, generous shelving and pivoting drawers.

Three years later came another house in the village for a teacher and her elderly mother. Here, it was decided to use brick and timber for external walls and concrete tiles for the roof, instead of the more expensive stone and cedar shingles. The frieze-like articulation of the upper, timber-clad storey, and the crisp

figure 5
The Round House, Ilmington, 1962, exterior.

figure 6
The Round House, Ilmington, 1962, detail of fireplace.

rectangular box of the house are reminiscent of Wright's Winslow House of 1893. However, the internal planning (which follows a more conventional pattern than in other houses designed by Harvey), and the exposed ceiling joists interspersed with deep shelves for the display of china ornaments, reveal a willingness to adapt to the client's tastes and needs.

In the 1960s Harvey designed a much more daring and sophisticated pair of houses in mid-Warwickshire. The first was designed for R.M. Wilson, a builder-client, in Cryfield Grange Road, between Coventry and Kenilworth, in 1965. Wilson was apparently not particularly interested in architecture, but wanted a house which would be noticed. The architects found this to be a liberating job because there was no interference in the design, as well as a generous budget. But at the same time they found it to be not a very profitable job, for Wilson used his own firm to build it, and it proved impossible to establish exactly what the building costs were, and therefore to calculate what was due in architects' fees. The main part of the house was at first-floor level, carried on a concrete slab, and consisted of an open-plan living room, dining and bar areas, a kitchen connected to the ground floor by an open staircase, sun-lounge, five bedrooms and a long balcony overlooking the garden at the rear. The ground floor contained a games room connected with the first floor by a semi-circular stone staircase, an indoor swimming pool and giant carport. Silver-grey Burma teak, used to clad the upper floor, provided an effective contrast with the roughcast Hornton stone of the ground floor.[22] Internally too, as a contemporary critic noted, colour and texture were employed to differentiate the two zones of this luxurious house:

"The ground floor is hard and virile, devoted to games, cars and swimming. The stones are tough, even forbidding, and the concrete parades its muscles. But the first floor is suave and open. The colours are soft and natural, the finishes are carefully designed and very sleek; it is a place of comfort and rest. Only the staircase remains to remind one of the hard world near at hand."[23]

The land falls away behind the house, giving splendid views from the balconies and garden. From this side of the house, although obscure glass screens separate the carport from the garden, cars are quite clearly visible, and appear as slightly menacing mechanical presences. The change of level means that the cars are raised up above the garden, where, apparently suspended between the house and the retaining wall of the terrace, they assume a dominance which is profoundly unsettling. Appropriately enough, Jaguar Cars used the house as the backdrop for publicity photographs designed to launch its XJS model.

22. The wood has now been varnished a rich brown, and the contrast in colour has unfortunately been lost.

23. G. Lewison and R. Billingham, *Coventry: New Architecture* (1969), p.96.

24. See 'Midland Houses: House for R.J. Povey Esq.', *Architecture West Midlands* no.22, Mar/April 1975, p.37.

25. Cedar Leys (illustrated Womersley, *op. cit.*, p.194), built in 1963 at Alveston. There is an interesting contemporary array of Wright-influenced houses by various architects in the locality: Roy Geden's Mistral, Kenilworth Road (1968); several ranch-style houses in Stoneleigh Road (1960s); and exuberant house conversions by Rex Chell, who practised in a Wrightian manner as a member of Coventry City Architects' department during the 1960s and early 1970s. By way of contrast, the influence of Mies can be detected in Cedar Leys and its two neighbours, and in 10 Eastfield Road, Leamington Spa (Hidalgo Moya, 1959, demolished 1987).

26. Povey was the owner of a dry cleaning business and apparently built the boiler himself.

27. At Tredington, Dr Lowe, who commissioned a retirement house from Harvey in 1978, had to agree to modifications to its design insisted on by a planning officer who said that the house should look as much like an artisan's dwelling as possible.

28. For example Keith Jones, who came to Coventry during the 1960s as Leisure Director of Mecca. He bought a house by H.N. Jepson at 7 Leighton Close, Coventry (built 1959) and then a house by Harvey at Abbey Fields, Kenilworth (built 1960), because he admired modern design and wanted large inter-communicating reception rooms for holding parties.

figure 7
House for a teacher, Ilmington, 1965.

The second house, designed in 1966–7 and built in 1969 at Barford, is set in a valley bottom, in five acres of river meadow dotted with mature trees and pools. The house is built on a bank, which was partly excavated for the bedroom wing; the main living area of the house was carried on a concrete slab above a carport and utility room and enjoys splendid views over the river.[24] As in the Wilson house, extensive use is made of mechanical devices; here they include a central-ised vacuum-cleaning system, warm-air heating and a panel gliding on tracks within the roof space, to cover an eight ft square skylight set into the living-room ceiling. In its use of concrete and glass to create a rectangular box poised over the landscape, the Barford house represents a simpler and bolder approach com-pared with the houses of just two years earlier. Tall Trees at Tredington and 9 Gibbet Hill Road – both designed by Harvey in 1963 – are far more discreet and ground hugging than the Barford house. Several distinguished Modern houses were being built near Stratford during the early 1960s, the most spectacular de-signed by Peter Womersley using an exposed concrete frame on a brick plinth,[25] which Harvey recalls visiting while it was under construction. Other factors which may have contributed to this aesthetic shift were the fact that the site at Barford was completely secluded, that the client was interested in engineering[26] and that the budget was a generous one.

During the 1970s Harvey built relatively few private houses, relying instead on commissions from Flowers and from the theatre and grammar school at Strat-ford. Harvey has attributed the curtailment of his work as domestic architect to the difficulty of gaining permission to build from planning authorities with fixed ideas of what was appropriate for rural sites.[27] He dates the beginning of a more assertive attitude on the part of planners around 1974. Harvey closed his office in Stratford in 1978, and continued his practice from home until his retirement in 1987.

Today, house-buyers regard Harvey's houses equivocally. They are acknowl-edged to be extremely well planned and comfortable; but to contemporary eyes they appear to offer too little in the way of accommodation in relation to the amount of land which they occupy. Their kitchens are regarded as rather small, and the gardens rather large for present-day tastes. The open-plan living spaces, which in the 1950s and 1960s were envisaged as appropriate to family life, have begun to lose their charm; today, as in the late-nineteenth century, there is a de-mand in affluent middle-class households for a series of separate rooms now dedicated to hobbies and the use of sophisticated electronic equipment. Inter-estingly, Harvey's houses are also perceived to be rather dark, with the result that some of the interior woodwork has been painted white or in pale colours.

The boxy, traditionally detailed houses which are presently being built on the southern approaches to Coventry suggest the interest of today's house-buyers in the symbolism of home, but attempt to satisfy it with a language of banal sim-

figure 8
South Winds (Wilson residence),
Cryfield Grange Road, Coventry, 1965,
exterior.

figure 9
South Winds (Wilson residence),
Cryfield Grange Road, Coventry, 1965,
view along first-floor balcony.

figure 10
South Winds (Wilson residence),
Cryfield Grange Road, Coventry, 1965,
dining room and sun lounge.

figure 11
House at Barford, 1969.

plicity. They form a stark contrast with houses nearby designed by Harvey in the 1960s, in which a sensitive approach to materials, an ingenious manipulation of room heights, of floor levels and interior spaces reveal his concern with the psychological and emotional aspects of domestic architecture. In his houses we find natural materials offset against man-made ones, generous fireplaces as well as invisible heating systems, productive gardens as well as sophisticated gadgetry. These dwellings possess a robust, almost homespun quality, as well as twentieth-century comforts which appealed strongly to the new elite of Coventry's postwar boom – the practical man of business, the engineer and retailer, the estate agent and the builder, who knew how to read plans and make things and demanded a high standard of design and construction in their own domestic envi-

ronments. Some of the individuals who commissioned them, like Wilson, and some of those who subsequently occupied them,[28] clearly wanted houses which projected a palpable aura of glamour, providing a sensuous display of natural and artificial materials, rough and glossy textures contained within a well-serviced and stoutly built cocoon. Interestingly, at the same time Harvey also achieved considerable success with a quite different, more elderly and often less extrovert type of client – namely the inhabitants of Ilmington and Tredington – who had become tired of living in draughty cottages or old rectories, and retired with relief to the Modern houses which he inserted for them into the fabric of their villages.

Nine houses in Suffolk by John Penn

RICHARD GRAY

Nine houses in Suffolk by John Penn

RICHARD GRAY

By the 1960s, the Modern Movement had won the battle against historicist styles; almost every architect in Britain became an adherent of the Modern Movement. Yet, in their domestic commissions, architects abandoned the white plaster walls of pre-war Continental Modernism, softening the revolutionary surfaces with various types of brickwork, that most traditional of British building materials. Modernism was still largely unfamiliar to the private client commissioning houses of modest size. During the 50s and 60s, Modernism only slowly crept up on them; large areas of glazing eventually became prevalent and the flat roof was accepted, despite the popular belief that it ill suited the British climate.

The clients of the architect John Penn, though, were always thoroughly convinced of the possibilities of Modern design. At least one had read widely on Modern architecture, from Corbusier to Frank Lloyd Wright. Another was familiar with the concept of *bureaulandschaft*[1] and more than content with the Miesian-style office block attached to his factory. Many of Penn's commissions came from retired people who wanted to live in rural surroundings or by the sea, while accepting modern design, some even with enthusiasm, who were unaware of the intellectual game being played out by Penn in the planning of their new homes.

Penn was schooled in the ways of the Modern Movement at the Architectural Association in the late 1940s, and, with greater intensity, during eighteen months working in Los Angeles for Richard Neutra. But on his return to Suffolk, Penn became interested less in the typical asymmetries of the Modern Movement house, than in what he has referred to as the 'temple-form plan'. The layout of his houses was conceived of as a metaphor for a classical temple, or, more specifically, inspired by the *megaron* – a hall in ancient Greece containing a central raised altar-like hearth, thought to be the ancestor of the Doric temple. Penn saw the hearth as a symbolic altar, around which a house could be planned. The centralised position of this feature dominated the planning, becoming a focus for the houses which dictated an all-embracing symmetry. Because of this rigorously symmetrical planning, Penn's houses have been referred to as Palladian, recalling the concentric layout of Palladio's mid-sixteenth-century north Italian villas, exploited by Lord Burlington and his circle in England during the second quarter of the eighteenth century. This Palladian villa plan often comprised a central hall surrounded by subsidiary rooms. Therefore the centre of a typical Penn house was dominated by a fireplace with a chimneystack attached to a service core of kitchen and bathrooms ('altar' or 'temple' type), or a hallway ('villa' type). In one instance he designed a house with a central internal courtyard – a feature possibly inspired by a very different source, the urban courtyard-house projects revitalised by the Bauhaus architects in the 1920s.

Penn's planning is remarkably fluent – undesirable long corridors are eliminated and space flows and circulates with ease. The facades of his houses were therefore predestined to be compositions of consummate formalism, particularly garden fronts, where a clear statement could be made uncluttered by the

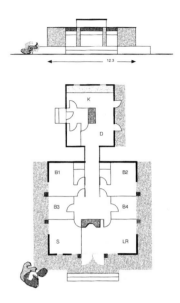

figure 1
Hasketon Lodge, exterior (opposite), elevation and plan.

1. Bureaulandschaft, literally, 'office landscape', in which traditional compartmentalised offices, created by the use of partitions, were replaced by an open working space.

figure 2
Bawdsey Hall Farm, exterior, elevation,
first and ground floor plans.

complexities of an entrance, and often expressed by a tripartite composition of brick piers and plate glass. Within the context of asymmetrical Modernism, where the facades of buildings are presumed to be governed by functional requirements, a pre-occupation with Classical or Palladian planning could be thought of as a romantic sentiment. The temple or Palladian planning formula served as a workable framework for Penn's houses, and provides an intriguing insight into an attempt to alloy two contrasting aesthetics. Contemporary journals[2] refer to Penn's interest in this classical planning concept as "laid out in formal Italian style".[3]

This article is concerned only with nine houses in Suffolk designed by Penn

 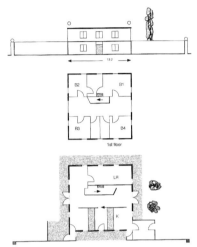

2. *Daily Mail Book of Bungalow Plans*, 1966–7.

3. A concern detectable at the time, when the Italian piazza was analysed in order to gain inspiration for the problems of urban renewal, as exemplified by Peter and Alison Smithson's planning of the Economist Building in St James's, London (1962–4), where the city block is 'exploded' and opened out to create a central piazza around which are grouped the various buildings. Penn, however, had no such thorny problem, as his houses were of modest size, many being only a single storey.

4. Penn was responsible for a number of works in the Woodbridge locality, as well as elsewhere, including his own homes. There were alterations to Little Haddon Hall (a substantial country house built in 1914 for a member of the Manners family); the conversion of the Old Lifeboat House at Shingle Street and the house in Woodbridge in which he now lives. The practice (Penn and his assistant Cedric Green) was also responsible for a factory at Framlingham – a glass and steel structure of Miesian directness. Further away was a sports pavilion for Penn's old college, Trinity, Cambridge, in collaboration with Christophe Grillet. Penn also had an interest in furniture design, and his unique triangular folding chair has been marketed with some success.

between 1962 and 1969, although they form part of a much larger corpus of work.[4]

In 1962, Penn designed a house for his mother in the grounds of Bawdsey Hall, the family home on the Suffolk coast. It was a requirement that Mrs Penn's existing furniture should fit into the new house and not look out of place, so conventional door apertures and windows were specified with no great expanses of glazing. At first glance the house could be mistaken for an early piece of Venturi-inspired Post-Modernism – a square brick cube with historicist references, such as the arched tops to the upper floor windows and, most obviously, the ball finials at each corner, which enlivened what would otherwise be an austere composition. Symmetrical walls flanking the entrance front screened the garden from the public gaze in the manner of the forecourt of an eighteenth-century Palladian country house. A broad central hallway bisected the ground and first floors, like the cross-hall of a Venetian palazzo. Sliding timber panels could close off the entrance lobby on the ground floor, altering the spatial configuration, and the axis of the cross-halls extended into the garden as an avenue of hornbeams.

Penn's next house, built in 1963 just outside Woodbridge, appeared to be an uncompromising piece of Modernism, especially on the garden front, but the facades were governed by a bi-laterally symmetrical plan, which also dictated the positioning of the garage on the entrance front. In this centralised 'altar' or 'temple' house, the service core, top lit by clerestory windows, made an appearance. Elsewhere in the house, clerestory glazing enhanced the spaciousness of the interiors, giving the impression that the solid walls were in fact moveable screens. The clerestory glazing may possibly have been derived from that in houses designed by Richard Neutra in the USA. The impact of the garden front has been blurred in recent years by the addition of a pergola festooned with foliage. In the following year, Penn used a plan similar to that of the Woodbridge house for one at Ufford, near Woodbridge, and again in 1965 for a house at Rendham, near Saxmundham, to achieve a fusion of classical symmetry with Modernist features; in the former, a hearth was again the focal point of the plan. It had two symmetrically positioned garages behind which, through the articulation of geometry involving the use of freestanding brick walls, sheltering courtyards were created. Clerestory mirrors endlessly reflected the boarded pine ceilings.

One of Penn's most interesting houses, built at Bruisyard in 1966, had a series of interconnecting spaces, arranged around a small central courtyard. Although single-storey courtyard houses are most effective in urban locations, with

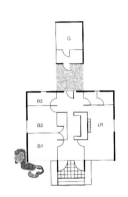

their inherent privacy, this house was built on an ample site and in a rural setting. The clients were enthusiasts for modern design, and they may well have come across similar houses in contemporary architectural journals. The commission may have been obtained through their friend Frederick Weinmann, one of Frederick Gibberd's assistants, with whom Penn had worked during the early days of Harlow New Town. In the Bruisyard house, the garden front was treated as a balancing tripartite composition, with symmetrical architectural elements on the other three sides. The plan indicates the movement of space, imperceptibly flowing from the sitting room – centrally positioned between the outside world and the inner sanctum of the courtyard – to the dining area and kitchen. In accordance with the architect's dictum of a central hearth, his preferred location for the fireplace would have been on the rear wall of the living room, backing onto the courtyard. The clients, however, rejected this suggestion, suggesting the fireplace be placed on the west wall of the living room, where it would not interrupt the glazing of the courtyard wall. Over 30 years later the same owners are still in occupation and the house has remained largely unaltered, although they have converted the courtyard into a conservatory by adding a glazed roof.

A year later the librettist Colin Graham commissioned a small house to be built near the coast at Orford. It had a large ground-floor living area but only one bedroom – guests were to be accommodated in an alcove opening off the living room. In the centre of the living space was a freestanding shrine-like stove. The bedroom, a symmetrically positioned superstructure on the first floor, was surrounded by a sunbathing terrace, shielded from the prevailing east wind by a weather-boarded fascia. The bedroom superstructure was also weatherboarded, a reference to a traditional component of East Anglian construction; the

figure 3
Garden House, Woodbridge.
Interior, elevation and plan.

figure 4
Elevation and plan of
Churchmeadow, Rendham.

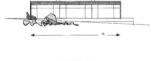

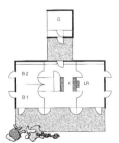

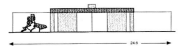

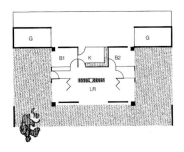

figure 5
Takoradi, Ufford, elevation and plan,
exterior and living room interior.

white-painted boarding indicates Penn's sensitivity to the proximity of the marine world.

Spectacularly sited facing the North Sea, and certainly one of the architect's most successful commissions, was the Beach House at Shingle Street, finally completed in 1972. Built as a summer retreat for his sister and brother-in-law, the house was for a short time actually occupied by Penn himself. Although an essay in formal bi-lateral planning and a Penn 'temple' house, it most embodied the 'freeing-up' process exerted on Penn by his years working in Southern California for Richard Neutra. While all the internal spaces still balanced one another, uses for the particular domains could be chosen at will, and sleeping areas were merely divided-off by lightweight folding doors. The main block of the house was a simple and lucid rectangle of white brick and glass, with a frieze below the roof of vertically-laid blue brick to delineate the composition. Guest accommodation was in a separate pavilion connected to one side of the entrance front by a wall and sheltering roof. Custom-made fibreglass panels, now lost, originally provided protection during winter for the huge expanse of vulnerable glazing.[5] Again, the internal walls of exposed brick stopped short of the ceiling, where horizontal clerestory mirrors enhanced the ceiling vistas and lightened the perceived mass. An amateur film made soon after the completion of the house conveys its relaxed atmosphere and something of the exceptional setting; sequences filmed inside reveal a sparsity of furniture in keeping with this ethereal marine residence. A model was also made of the house. Recently the present owners, who live in the house all year round rather than for weekends and holidays, have connected the main block to the guest pavilion by a hallway, thereby nullifying the architect's original conception.

Typical of Penn's houses in the temple/Palladian genre and is one commissioned by a Mrs Louge at Hasketon near Woodbridge, built in 1961. It stood on a podium of Suffolk white bricks, which not only contained storage space, but also lifted the main living rooms clear above the flat surroundings – the grounds of a demolished country house – adding a touch of grandeur and creating a terrace from which the park could be approached by way of imposing steps arranged on the main axis, as with the *piano nobile* of a Palladian villa. Louvered ventilation apertures with arched tops were built into the plinth, a reference to the nineteenth-century block attached to the rear, a former gate lodge, and subtly implying that Penn's new pavilion was mounted on something older. An additional window

5. Patrick Betts, the maker of these fibreglass panels, later commissioned a factory at Framlingham.

(for the study) compromised the balance of the principal garden facade, but the two return fronts were identical with symmetrical tripartite windows, demonstrating the architect's overriding pre-occupation with this concern. Internally, the rooms were grouped around a central top-lit hall, an arrangement derived from Palladio.

In 1969 Penn designed a two-storey house overlooking a bird sanctuary on the Westleton marshes near Dunwich, the medieval city lost to the North Sea. Permission to build in this sensitive location could only be obtained by maintaining to the local authority that a farmhouse was required. The client, Peter Youngman, had an interest in modern architecture and gave his architect a free rein. With the main axis measuring almost eighteen metres in length, the house was larger than most of Penn's other commissions. A steep bank at the rear of the site had to be excavated to create a level terrace for building. Inside the house there was much exposed brickwork: blue engineering bricks, with a curved profile, were laid as a threshold for the huge sliding windows on the principal garden front. Originally, all the accommodation was at ground level, with the first floor intended as an immense apple loft (to comply with the agricultural planning permission), which consequently required few windows and was reached by an iron spiral stair. As ever, at the centre of the plan lay a hearth, facing the view of the bird sanctuary, the latter being of particular interest to Peter Youngman's wife, Diana, an enthusiastic ornithologist. Behind the hearth lay the kitchen, which always suffered from insufficient light, resulting from the arrangement of the small square windows dictated by the symmetry of the entrance facade. Internal clerestory glazing and horizontal high-level mirrors were once again employed here to extend the perspective effect of the cedar-board ceilings. In recent years, the apple loft in the upper floor has been colonised for extra sleeping quarters and a workroom, with the result that two more windows have been introduced on the main garden front, thereby impairing the crescendo effect of the original

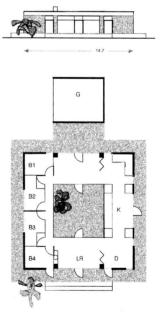

figure 6
Sartoria, Bruisyard, exterior, living room looking through to the internal courtyard, elevation and plan.

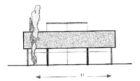

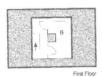

figure 7
Lion House, Orford, exterior,
elevation, first floor and ground
floor plans.

6. *Houses and Bungalows*, Batsford, London,
1958 and *Houses for Today*, Batsford, London
1971.

7. John Entenza, the publisher and editor of the
American journal *Arts & Architecture* conceived
this highly influential scheme. The project, in
Los Angeles, to construct a series of small but
architecturally advanced houses, was announced in January 1945, seven months short of the
end of World War II. Established Californian
practices such as that of Richard Neutra and
Charles Eames were invited to submit designs,
together with what were then relatively
unknown architects, including Raphael
Soriano, Pierre Koenig and Craig Ellwood; the
scheme secured the reputations of this younger
generation of architects. Most spectacular were
their long, sleek exercises in steel and glass
perched on the arid and rocky Los Angeles
mountains, as revealed in the elegant photography of Julius Shulman.

design. Uncluttered and simply furnished to begin with, heavy traditional furniture which is unsuitable for such interiors has since accrued.

What can we make of Penn's houses today? June Park's contemporary books on small, one-off Modern houses[6] reveal no other British architect quite so immersed in planning conundrums of such complexity, although Bauhaus-style courtyard houses were not unknown: there were examples of the type by Frishman and Spyer in Hampstead, Leonard Manessah at Reigate and Michael Manser at Leatherhead. The service core appears in their various schemes too and is included in a prototype steel-framed house by Richard Rogers. In the USA, however, rigorously symmetrical houses occur in the work of several East Coast architects and, like Penn's work, they remained resolutely Modern, with no retreat into historicism. The most well-known name to engage himself with this notion was Philip Johnson, whose house for a television executive at New Canaan, Connecticut (designed in association with Landis Gores) had a symmetrical plan and incorporated an internal courtyard. But another house in Connecticut, designed by a less-familiar name, John Johansen, had pavilions at each corner – like Kent's Holkham Hall – and most adequately demonstrated a plan inspired by Palladio – if not Greek antecedents. The American journal, *Architectural Record*, refers to this single-storey house constructed in 1958, as an example of 'disciplined romanticism' and mentions that 'a rational, regulated neo-Palladian influence dominates the plan and balanced design'. The glazed central area of this substantial and luxurious residence housed the living rooms, while each wing contained other functions: one for the kitchen, laundry and servants' accommodation, another as a master-bedroom suite, one for family bedrooms and the fourth as a guest pavilion (also intended to double as a study) with its own private courtyard. Total adherence to symmetry was abandoned, as the guest/study pavilion was smaller than the other wings: neither is the order of the fenestration symmetrical – one can, in fact, look at the plan as being merely a sensible way of zoning functions. Other American architects also experimented with planning to a strict grid – equivalent to Penn's work is a house designed in 1957 by Ulrich Franzen in Rye, New York State, in which the accommodation was organised through the use of uncompromising symmetry, dictating the position of the windows and door apertures. Franzen's house also has similar Neutra-style clerestory windows extending along the tops of the walls.

Apart from the implications of basing his house plans on ancient Greek precedents, the influence of American Modernism propounded by the Los Angeles Case Study House scheme of the late 1940s,[7] can also be appreciated in Penn's

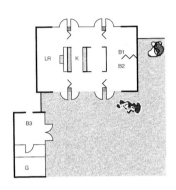

facades (particularly in the single-storey projects, which is also, of course, true of many British architects working in the genre at the time). In 1950s Britain, the steel of these Californian precursors was in short supply; architects here were forced to fall back on the less stylish but cheaper brick, and Penn, in Suffolk, embraced this homely but honourable material. While also employing indigenous shingles, Penn's expansive areas of glazing would not have disgraced a Koenig or Neutra eyrie overlooking the plain of Los Angeles.

John Penn's contribution to Modern domestic architecture can be seen as an attempt to fuse function with a poetic re-interpretation of formalism, within the discipline of building on a modest scale. Here, order provided an architectural matrix for Penn's work; it connected a peculiarly introspective concern for a plan both derived from the *megaron* and with a subconscious deference to the Palladian villa, to that of Californian spontaneity. It is not difficult to be seduced by the nostalgia of this appealing and romantic idea, namely, to allow the exquisite control of a particular past to ordain the shape of what, in effect, is a Modern concept. Penn's use of romantic and poetic inspiration from classical precedents as the basis of planning resolutely Modern structures, surely makes his work of interest, and deserving of much wider recognition.

figure 8
Beach House, Shingle Street, exterior views (this page & opposite bottom), interior, elevation and plan.

figure 9
Fenstreet, Westleton, exterior, elevation, first floor and ground floor plans.

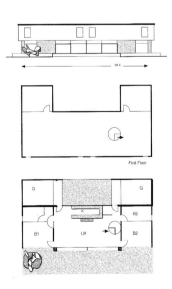

I would like to thank the architect for kindly allowing me to interview him for the preparation of this article. My thanks also go to James Coote, professor of Architecture at the University of Austin, Texas, for additional assistance.

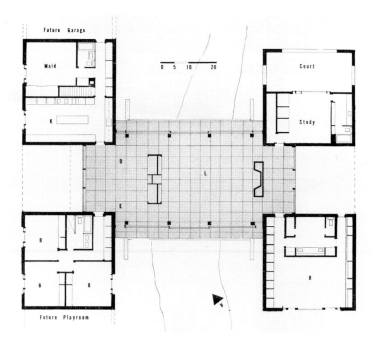

figure 10
House in Connecticut
by John Johansen, plan.
(British Architectural Library,
RIBA, London)

7 List of architect-designed houses in England 1945–1975

MATTHEW HARDY

List of architect-designed houses in England 1945–1975

MATTHEW HARDY

This list of houses is only the first step towards a more complete documentary record, and its limitations should be understood. It has been assembled from a variety of sources, few of which can claim objectivity or completeness.

The criterion for defining a house has been a single building, whether freestanding or not. Some small groups of houses of exceptional interest have been included, but larger speculative developments have not.

The fact that a house is designed by an architect has normally been a sine-qua-non, but 'architect' is not strictly defined, and some houses are by designers of other kinds.

No explicit criteria of style have been applied. In this, the list differs from the Gazetteer of Modern Houses, 1919–1939 by Jeremy Gould, as printed in *Twentieth Century Architecture 2: The Modern House Revisited* (1996). Gould takes the flat roof as the basic criterion for inclusion (although there are exceptions). For the post-war period, no such simple identification marks apply, and the present list is as stylistically plural as possible, including classical houses and a few castles.

The list covers England, with some entries for Scotland and Wales. The end date of 1975 has not been rigorously applied, but indicates a lull in new house building owing to economic circumstances, and a moment when planning controls began to make the erection of modern houses more difficult.

There have been no intentional criteria of architectural quality, but since the majority of examples are taken from published sources, this implies some initial filtering process. It is very likely, nonetheless, that some important and interesting houses have been omitted. The private nature of private houses has meant that information about their existence has often not been publicly available. Furthermore, typical houses of this time are invisible from public roads. It is important, therefore, that absence from this list should not, at any time, be taken necessarily to imply inferior quality. Readers should understand that inclusion in the present list does not imply any right of access.

Demolitions have been recorded where known, and severe cases of alteration. Decisions on the inclusion of alterations and additions to earlier houses have been reached pragmatically, with major works included.

No list of this type has ever been prepared before, however, and if it has many holes, it may at least act like a cellular blanket to warm up the subject. The post-war period was probably the most varied and fertile for individual house design in the whole history of British architecture, and a start needed to be made somewhere.

The list has been compiled by Matthew Hardy, using source material supplied by Alan Powers and Bronwen Edwards, originally assembled in the process of listing research for English Heritage, and further additions have been made by Elain Harwood and by individual architects who responded to a public appeal for information. The Twentieth Century Society welcomes additions to the list (preferably accompanied by photographs and outline information), so that a revised list can be published in due course.   AP

Abbreviations

JOURNALS

A	Architect
ABN	The Architect and Building News
AD	Architectural Design
Ad'A	Architecture d'Aujourd'hui
ADC	Architectural Design and Construction (later Architectural Design)
AEM	Architect East Midlands
AJ	Architect's Journal
ANW	Architect North West
AR	Architectural Review
A&U	Architecture & Urbanism (Tokyo)
AWM	Architect West Midlands
Br	Builder
Bldg	Building
BB	Brick Bulletin
BD	Building Design
BM	Baumeister
B&W	Bauen und Wohnen (Munich)
CL	Country Life
CQ	Concrete Quarterly
DBZ	Deutsche Bauzeitung
GH	Good Housekeeping
HB	House Builder
H&G	House & Garden
ID	Interior Design
IdC	Informes de la Construccion
IH	Ideal Home
MJeMM	Mon Jardin et Ma Maison
NA	Northern Architect
NT	The National Trust Magazine
PA	Progressive Architecture
RIBAJ	RIBA Journal
TB	The Builder
WJ	Women's Journal
YA	Yorkshire Architect

BOOKS

Place of publication is London unless noted otherwise

Archer 1985	Lucy Archer, Raymond Erith, Architect, Burford, 1985
Aslet & Powers 1985	Clive Aslet & Alan Powers, The National Trust Book of the English House, 1985
BofE/BoW/BoS Pevsner	Buildings of England; Buildings of Wales; Buildings of Scotland, various dates
Booth & Taylor 1970	Philip Booth & Nicholas Taylor, Cambridge New Architecture 1970
Brogden 1986	W.A. Brogden, Aberdeen, an illustrated architectural guide, Edinburgh 1986
Bruckmann & Lewis 1960	Hansmartin Bruckmann & David Lewis Neuer Wohnbau in England, Stuttgart 1960
Cantacuzino 1964	Sherban Cantacuzino, Modern Houses of the World, 1964
Cantacuzino 1981	Sherban Cantacuzino, Howell Killick Partridge & Amis: architecture, 1981
Clifford & Enthoven 1954	H. Dalton Clifford and R.E. Enthoven, New Homes from Old Buildings, 1954
Clifford 1957	H. Dalton Clifford, New Houses for Moderate Means, 1957
Clifford 1963	H. Dalton Clifford, Houses for Today, 1963
Dannatt 1972	Trevor Dannatt, Trevor Dannatt: buildings and interiors 1951/72, 1972
DC	Design Centre publications, authors as noted
Dunnett & Stamp 1983	James Dunnett and Gavin Stamp, Ernö Goldfinger, 1983
Edwards 1995	Brian Edwards, Basil Spence 1907–1976, Edinburgh, 1995
Einzig 1981	Einzig, Richard, Classic Modern Houses in Europe, 1981
Emanuel 1980	Muriel Emanuel (ed.), Contemporary Architects, 1980
Foster 1991	Norman Foster, Team 4 and Foster Associates Buildings and Projects, Vol.I '1964–73', 1991
Gilliat 1966	Mary Gilliat, English Style, 1966
Gowan 1994	James Gowan, Style & Configuration, 1994
Gresswell 1964	Peter Gresswell, Houses in the Country, 1964
Gwynne nd	Patrick Gwynne, Houses by Patrick Gwynne 1938–1979
Harling 1961	Robert Harling (ed.), House and Garden Book of Small Houses, 1961
Harling 1963	Robert Harling (ed.), House & Garden Book of Cottages, 1963
Harling 1968	Robert Harling (ed.), House & Garden Book of Holiday and Weekend Houses, 1968
Harwood & Powers 1998	Alan Powers & Elain Harwood, Tayler and Green Architects 1938–1973, 1998
Harwood 2000	Elain Harwood, England: A guide to post-war listed buildings, 2000
Herts 1979	Hertfordshire Association of Architects, Architecture in Herts 1929–1979 (exh. cat.), 1979
Hope 1963	Alice Hope, Town Houses, 1963
Jackson 1996	Neil Jackson, The Modern Steel House, 1996
Jones & Woodward 1992	Edward Jones & Christopher Woodward, A Guide to the Architecture of London, 1992
Lambert 1963	Sam Lambert (ed.), New Architecture of London, A Selection of Buildings Since 1930, 1963
Lowrie 1974	Joyce Lowrie, Modern Houses in Town and Country, 1974
Martin 1983	Leslie Martin, Buildings & Ideas 1933–83 from the Studio of Leslie Martin and his Associates, 1983
Mauger 1959	Paul Mauger, Buildings in the Country, 1959
McKean & Jestico 1976	Charles McKean & Tom Jestico (eds.) Guide to Modern Buildings in London 1965–75, 1976
McKean 1982	Charles McKean, Architectural Guide to Cambridge and East Anglia Since 1920, Edinburgh, 1982
McKean & Walker 1984	Charles McKean and David Walker, Dundee, an illustrated introduction, Edinburgh, 1984
Mills 1953	Edward D. Mills, New Architecture in Great Britain, 1953
Murray & Trombley 1990	Peter Murray & Stephen Trombley, ADT Modern Architecture Guide – Britain, 1990
Nairn 1964	Ian Nairn, Modern Buildings in London, 1964
Newton 1992	Miranda Newton, Architects' London Houses, 1992
Park 1958	June Park, Houses and Bungalows, 1958
Park 1971	June Park, Houses for Today, 1971
Penn 1954	Colin Penn, Houses of To-day, A Practical Guide, 1954
Pidgeon & Crosby 1960	Monica Pidgeon & Theo Crosby, An Anthology of Houses, 1960
Powell 1995	Kenneth Powell, Edward Cullinan Architects, 1995
Powell 1999	Kenneth Powell, Richard Rogers Complete Works I, 1999
Powers 1987	Alan Powers, H.S. Goodhart-Rendel, Architect 1887–1959, 1987
Powers 1989	Alan Powers, Oliver Hill, Architect and lover of life, 1989
Powers 1992	Alan Powers, In the Line of Development: F.R.S. Yorke, E. Rosenberg & C.S. Mardall to YRM 1930–1992, 1992
Powers 1999	Alan Powers, Francis Pollen Architect 1926–87, 1999
Robinson 1984	John Martin Robinson, The Latest Country Houses, 1984
Rowe (ed) 1984	Colin Rowe (ed.), James Stirling, Buildings and Projects, 1984
Sandon 1977	Eric Sandon, Suffolk Houses, 1977
Sharp 1966	Dennis Sharp, (ed.) Manchester Buildings, An Architecture North West Publication, 1966
Smith & Marks	David Smith & Godfrey Marks, New Oxford, Oxford, n.d.
Stephen 1965	Douglas Stephen, Kenneth Frampton, & Michael Carapetian, British Buildings, 1960–64, 1965
Synthesis 1994	Peter Stead et al, Synthesis, art + architecture, projects in collaboration, 1954–1994, Huddersfield, 1994
Taylor 1970	Nicholas Taylor, Cambridge New Architecture, 1970
Walter 1955/7	Felix Walter (ed.), Fifty Modern Bungalows, 1955; Second revised edition, 1957
Whiting 1964	Penelope Whiting, New Houses, London, 1964
Willis 1977	Peter Willis, New Architecture in Scotland, 1977
Wolfe 1959	Rainer Wolfe, Das kleine Haus, 1959
Wolseniger 1968	Bernard Wolseniger, Maisons de Vacances in Europe, Fribourg, 1968

Alphabetical listing by architect

Ahm, Povl, see Utzon, Jørn

Ahrends, Burton and Koralek

▸ Dunstan Road, Old Headington, Oxford
AR Jan 1966 p.50
AR Sept 1970 p.188
CQ Oct–Dec 1971 pp.22–3
Ad'A Dec 1971–Jan 1972 pp.68–70
HB vol.33 no.5 May 1973 p.279

▸ Bryan-Brown house, Thurleston, Devon, 1964
Emanuel 1980 p.17

Aldington, Peter

▸ Askett Green, Crowbrook Road, Askett, Aylesbury, Bucks, 1962–3
Whiting 1964 pp.91–97
Harwood 2000 5.32
Listed grade II

▸ Three houses: The Turn, Middle Turn, Turn End (own house), Townside, Haddenham, Aylesbury, Bucks HP17 8BG, 1963–4
AR Aug 1968 pp.102–4
CQ July–Sept 1968
Park 1971
Einzig 1981
Harwood 2000 5.46
Listed grade II

▸ House at Doncaster, 1968
AR Aug 1972 pp.89–92

▸ 'Diggs Field', Haddenham, Bucks, 1964
D-Extrakt vol.8 June 1971
IH Nov 1971 pp.52–5
RIBAJ July 1970 p.302
AR 1968 pp.102–4
AJ 2 Sept 1970 pp.532–6
A&U 1971 no.7 pp.21–25

▸ Clayton house, Prestwood, Bucks, 1964–6
DBZ (Stuttgart) Mar 1971 pp.266–7
AR Aug 1971 pp.76–80
Harwood 2000 5.48
Listed grade II

▸ (Aldington and Craig)
Anderton house, 'Rigg Side', Goodleigh, Barnstaple
AJ 28 Feb 1973 pp.491–504
AJ 25 Apr 1973 pp.997–998
DBZ 1973 pp.641–3
AJ 22 Aug 1973 pp.445–6
H&G June 1973 pp.106–9
Harwood 2000 4.28
Listed grade II*

Allan, Gordon

▸ 112 Camphill Road, Dundee
McKean & Walker 1984 p.112

Allen, William A.

▸ Own house, 4 Ashley Close, Welwyn Garden City, Herts, 1948
McKean 1982 p.182

▸ (with Bickerdike, John)
J.D.A. Boyd house, 8 Ashley Close, Welwyn Garden City, Herts, c.1953
H&G Sept 1953 pp.45–7, 87
McKean 1982 p.182

Architects Co-Partnership

▸ (Kenneth Capon)
Own house, 'Wildwood Cottage', 17 North End, London NW3, 1950–1, 1955
AJ 20 Sept 1951
Penn 1954 p.130
Daily Mail Ideal Home Book 1956 pp.29–33

▸ (Leo de Syllas)
P. de Syllas house, 4 The Glade, Welwyn Garden City, Herts, 1951
H&G July 1952 pp.34–7, 84
Penn 1954 pp.92, 155
McKean 1982 p.182

▸ (Kenneth Capon)
Own holiday house, Upper Wolves Copse, Bosham Hoe, nr Chichester Harbour, W. Sussex, 1955–6
H&G Feb 1956 pp.64–5 (kitchen only)
H&G May 1956 pp.72–3
Clifford 1957 p.52
Harling 1961 pp.74–5

▸ House at The Reddings, Welwyn Garden City, Herts, 1955
Walter 1955/7 pp.18–19

▸ House at Ham, Richmond, Surrey, 1955
Walter 1955/7 pp.22–3

▸ (Anthony Cox)
Own house, 5 Bacon's Lane, Highgate, 1957

▸ (Peter Cocke)
Own house, 1–2 Bacon's Lane, Highgate, 1958

▸ (Kenneth Capon)
'Salt Hill', Bridle Way, Grantchester, Cambs 1959
McKean 1982 p.41

▸ (Michael Powers)
Own house, 3 Heath Side, Hampstead, 1959

▸ (Michael Powers)
The President's House, Corpus Christi College, Oxford, 1959

▸ (Michael Powers)
Houses for St John's College, nos.15–17 (odd) Blackhall Road, Oxford, 1963
Whiting 1964 pp.40–7
BofE Oxfordshire 1974 p.315
Harwood 2000 5.40
Listed grade II

Arup Associates

▸ (Philip Dowson)
Own studio house at Monks Eleigh, Suffolk, 1959
McKean 1982 p.106

▸ (Philip Dowson and Peter Foggo)
S.V. Williams house 'Long Wall', Newman's Green, Long Melford, Suffolk, 1962–4
CL 25 Feb 1965 pp.432–3
Whiting 1964 pp.114–17
ERA May–June 1971 p.19
Cantacuzino 1964
Emanuel 1980 p.213
McKean 1982 p.106
Harwood 2000 3.86
Listed grade II

▸ (Philip Dowson)
House at 2a Drax Avenue, London SW20, 1965–9
McKean & Jestico 1976 p.65
Emanuel 1980 p.213

▸ House at Merton, Wimbledon
AR Aug 1972 pp.83–8

Austin-Smith Lord

▸ 89 Barton Road, Cambridge, 1975
McKean 1982 p.44

Ball, Donald

▸ House at Chislehurst, Kent
AR Aug 1968 p.109
H&G Apr 1969 pp.86–9

Banks, Gerald

▸ Own house, Witney, Oxon, 1954
Clifford 1957 pp.36–7

▸ House at Witney, Oxon, 1954
Clifford 1957 pp.38–9

▸ Odell Castle, Bedfordshire, for 2nd Lord Luke, 1962
Robinson 1984 p.221

▸ House for Merton College, Savile Road, opp. New College School, Oxford
Smith & Marks (nd) n.p.

Barefoot, Peter

▸ Silver house, Quay Street, Orford, Suffolk, 1964

Barnes, Harry S.

▸ Own house at Chadwick Lane, Heywood, Lancs, 1953
Walter 1955/7 pp.86–7

Barr, Cleeve

▸ Barr house, nr Box Hill, Leatherhead, Surrey, 1953
H&G Feb 1956 pp.52–5
Penn 1954 pp.48, 50
Clifford 1957 pp.40–1

Bartlett, K.

▸ House at Horton-cum-Studley, Oxford
Interbuild June 67 pp.24–6

Bartlett and Fairweather

▸ House for Christopher Taylor, London
H&G May 1972 pp.94–5

Bartlett & Gray

▸ Abbeywood House, Newstead Abbey, Nottingham, 1954–6
H&G 1958
Park 1958 p.140
Harling 1961 pp.50–1
BofE Nottinghamshire

Barton, John

▸ Surgeon Pearson house, Epping Forest, Essex, c.1954
H&G Aug 1954 pp.32–5, 77

Bayley, A.C.

▸ Colentina, Addington, Surrey, 1954–5
BofE Surrey p.89

Bazeley, Geoffrey and Barbary

▶ Agricultural worker's cottage, nr Penzance, Cornwall, 1949
Clifford 1957 p.42

▶ House nr Cambourne, Cornwall, 1954
Clifford 1957 p.43

Beckett, Sir Martyn

▶ Own house Kirkdale Farm, Kirkdale, N. Yorks, 1952
Clifford 1963 pp.22–4
Robinson 1984 p.215

▶ Southfield House, Chawton, Hampshire, for Sir Richard Sharples, 1956
Robinson 1984 pp.226–7

▶ Callernich, N. Uist, 1962
Robinson 1984 pp.120, 204

▶ Herriard Park, Hampshire, for J.L. Jervoise, 1970
Robinson 1984 p.212

▶ Swarcliffe Hall, West Yorkshire, for Col. B.C. Greenwood, c.1970
Robinson 1984 p.228

▶ Neasham Hall, Co. Durham, for Sir John Wrightson Bt, 1971
Robinson 1984 pp.122, 220

Bell, Peter & Partners (with MacCormac & Jamieson)

▶ (Peter Bell and Richard MacCormac) House at 4a Langton Way, London SE3, 1974
McKean & Jestico 1976 p.70

Belsom, David

▶ Own house, Stock, Essex
H&G July 1965

Beech, Gerald

▶ 'Green Haddon', Turner's Hill Road and Coombe Hill Road, East Grinstead, E. Sussex, 1961–2

▶ House in Ham Farm Road, Ham, Richmond-on-Thames, 1956

▶ House at Grange Corner (Callis Court Road and Grange Road), Broadstairs, Kent, 1963

Beech, Gerald and Dewi Prys Thomas

▶ 'Cedarwood', 50 Beaconsfield Road, Woolton, Liverpool, 1960
(Women's Journal House of the Year 1960)
WJ March 1960 pp.20–37
AJ 3 March 1960 p.381
AR March 1960 pp.153–4

Bemlow, Kenneth (of Cluttons)

▶ Bayham Manor, Kent, for 5th Marquess of Camden, c.1973
Robinson 1984 p.201

▶ Saxonbury House, Frant, Kent, for Lord Roderic Pratt, 1970s
Robinson 1984 p.225

▶ Dower house, Somerley, Hampshire, for Fiona, Countess of Northampton, c.1970
Robinson 1984 p.226

Berry, Dennis (with Henry Goddard)

▶ House at Penenden Heath, Maidstone, Kent, 1955
H&G July 1956 pp.60–3
Walter 1955/7 pp.50–1

Binns, G.R.

▶ Own house, Hutton, Essex, 1955
Walter 1955/7 pp.104–5
Clifford 1957 p.44

Bickerdike, John

▶ House at 11 The Reddings, Welwyn Garden City, Herts, 1955
McKean, 1982, p.182

▶ Bickerdike, John – see also entry under Allen, William

Bird, T.A.

▶ House at Hampstead, London NW3, 1952
Clifford 1957 pp.46–7

Blanc, Alan & Sylvia

▶ Own house, (Uphill House), Coombe Hill Road, Kingston-on-Thames, 1957–60
Newton 1992, pp.26–31

Blomfield, Giles

▶ Own house, Lanterglas, Calerick, Truro, Cornwall
Br 22 Oct 1965 p.869
Br 21 Jan 1966 pp.122–3
ABN 16 Sept 1964 pp.543–6
IH 1966 pp.19–23

Bloom, Victor

▶ Own house, Elstree, Herts, 1953
Clifford 1957 p.48

Blundell-Jones, Peter & Gillian Smith

▶ Blundell-Jones house, Culm Vale, Stoke Canon, Devon, 1976–7
BofE Devon p.763

Board, R. Vyvyan

▶ Own house, Batson, near Selcombe, Dorset
H&G Nov 1954 pp.62–5, 120

Boissevain, Paul & Osmond, Barbara

▶ Charles Howkins house 'Thirteen', Admiral's Walk, London NW3, 1958
Hope 1963 pp.75–82

▶ Split-level weekend house nr Dorking, Surrey, 1958
Harling 1961 pp.64–5

▶ House at Walton-on-the-Hill, c.1958
Harling 1961 pp.34–5

▶ 'Redings', Totteridge, Middlesex, 1961–2
BofE London IV p.190

Bonnington, John S.

▶ Own house 'Ferrum House', Grange Court Road, Harpenden, Herts, 1961–3
(Ideal Home House of the Year 1964)
IH Sept 1964
Artecase Sept Oct 1964
AD May 1965 pp.257–8
B&W Dec 1965 no.12 pp.481–4
ABN 22 Sept 1965 pp.538–44
GH Jan 1966
H&G Sept 1966 pp.66–71
MJeMM Nov 1966
AJ 2 Sept 1970 pp.527–31
Herts 1979 p.33
BofE Herts (2nd ed) pp.45, 158
DC Goulden, Gontron, 'Bathrooms'
DC Phillips, Derek, 'Lighting'
DC Meade, Dorothy, 'Bedrooms'
Wolfe 1959
Harwood 2000 3.88
Listed grade II

Booth & Ledeboer

▶ House at Wimbledon, Surrey, c.1953
Penn 1954 pp.30, 40

Booton and Farmer

▶ 'Patch House', Main Street, Heslington, York
YA Mar/Apr 1969 pp.100–1

Bostock, Robert of Bostock & Wilkins

▶ 'Broadleaze', Boyton, Wiltshire, for Raymond Wheatley-Hubbard, 1963
Robinson 1984 p.203

Boston, Peter – see entry under James and Bywaters

Bowyer, Gordon and Ursula

▶ House at Grantham, Lincs
AD Jan 1957 pp.10–11
AR Feb 1957 pp.119–20

▶ Two houses at Blackheath, London SE3 (one for Dennis Healey MP)
Pidgeon & Crosby 1960 pp.89–91
Harling 1961 pp.82–3

Boys Jarvis Partnership (Anthony Cicalese)

▶ James McKelvie house, 'Shambala', Trumpet Hill, Gourock, Renfrewshire, 1968
Willis 1977 pp.22–3

Branch, David

▶ Branch house, Meadowbank, Blackheath, Greenwich, 1970
Newton 1992 pp.76–81

Bradshaw, Gass & Hope (Robert McNaught)

▶ House at Lowstock, Bolton, Lancs

Bradshaw, W.T. – see entry under Browne, Lloyd and Partners

Brawne, Michael

▶ Own house at 31 South Hill Park, London NW3, 1961
AR Nov 1961 pp.345–7
Lambert 1963 p.70
Hope 1963 pp.33–7
Whiting 1964 pp.138–43
Emanuel 1980 p.115
Jones & Woodward 1992 p.51

▶ House at Fisher's Pond, Winchester, Hants, 1967
AR Dec 1967 pp.458–60
CQ Apr–June 1969 pp.38–40
H&G Nov 1969 pp.58–61
DBZ Oct 1972 p.1071
Emanuel 1980 p.117
Wolseniger 1968
Lowrie 1974

Brett, Lionel

▶ House at Taidswood, Iver Heath, Bucks, 1954
Walter 1955/7 pp.40–2

Brett, Lionel (Brett, Boyd & Bosanquet)

▶ Hans Juda house, Fawley Bottom, nr Henley-on-Thames, Chilterns, Oxon, c.1957
Harling 1961 pp.62–3
Harling 1968 pp.76–9

Brett, Lionel (Brett & Pollen)

▶ Lord Dormer house 'Grove Park', Hampton on the Hill, Warks, 1964
Powers 1999 p.73

Brett, Lionel (Brett & Pollen)

▶ Own house, Christmas Common, Oxfordshire
AR Aug 1968 pp.100–1
Park, 1971, pp.109–10

Brewster, David

▶ House at 10 Chancery Place, The Green, Writtle, Essex

Brock, David

▶ Aderne Hall, Cheshire, c.1975
Robinson 1984 p.198

Brockbank, Russell

▶ House in garden of Badgers, The Lane, Thursley, Surrey, 1953
BofE Surrey p.486

Brown, Neave

▶ Terrace, 24–32 (even) Winscombe Street, London N19, 1964–5
(Own house no.30)
AD July 1968 pp.330–4
Zodiac (Milan) no.18 pp.84–7
Newton 1992 pp.58–65

Browne, Lloyd and Partners (Bradshaw, W.T.)

▶ Own house, Knaresborough, Yorks
YA Mar–Apr 1969 pp.99

Building Design Partnership

▶ Three houses, Hornby, Lancs
Bldg 23 Aug 1972 pp.23–5

Building Design Partnership (Ingham, Keith)
▸ Keith Ingham house, Lytham, Lancs, 1968 and later extension
AJ 26 August 1970 pp.473–6
H&G June 1969 pp.70–3
ANW Dec 63–Jan 64 p.44
Park, 1971, pp.63–5

Building Design Partnership (David Keate)
▸ Keate house, 7 Trafalgar Road, Cambridge

Bulmer, Harold, and J. Ricardo Pearce
▸ House at Raynes Park, London, 1953
Walter 1955/7 p.64

Burton, Michael
▸ Friezland House, High Hoyland, Yorks 1959
ABN Sept 1959 pp.336–8
▸ Place House, Kingston Langley,Chippenham, Wilts, c.1968

Butler, A.S.G.
▸ Lessingham Manor, Norfolk, for W. Neave, 1945
Robinson 1984 p.216
▸ Bourne Wood, Hampshire for Col Kinglake Tower, 1956
CL 11 Dec 1958
Robinson 1984 pp.61, 202

Buzas, Stefan – see entry under Cubitt, James and Partners

Cadbury-Brown, H.T.
▸ Own house, 3 Church Walk, Aldeburgh 1964–5
Gilliat 1966
Sandon 1977 p.333
CL 2 Oct 1997, pp.52–57
▸ Imogen Holst house, Church Walk, Aldeburgh 1964–5

Cambridge Design Group (David Thurlow)
▸ Houses at Water Lane, Histon, Cambs, 1972
H&G Oct 1971 pp.109–11
AR Aug 1971 pp.94–6
McKean 1982 p.43
▸ Own house, 1 Old Pound Yard, Histon, Cambs, 1973
H&G Dec 1973–Jan 1974 pp.86–91
McKean 1982 p.44

Cantacuzino, Sherban
▸ House at East Brabourne, Kent, 1953
Clifford 1957 p.49

Cantacuzino, Sherban – see entry for Stean, Shipman & Cantacuzino

Carter, Bertram
▸ Punnett's Town (house and surgery), Heathfield, E. Sussex, 1950–1
Penn 1954 p.141
BofE Sussex p.531

Carter and Salaman
▸ House at Steep, nr Petersfield, Hants, 1955
Clifford 1957 pp.50–1

Cassidy, Michael
▸ Own house, Yapton Road, Barnham, W. Sussex, 1974

Casson, Sir Hugh & Conder, Neville & Partners
▸ House at 10 Cathcart Road, Kensington, 1953–4 extended by Timothy Rendle as Fig Tree Cottage, c.1964
H&G Mar 1955 pp.70–1
AR Nov 1964 pp.357–9
Hope 1963 pp.116–8

Casson, Sir Hugh, and Casson, Margaret, and Green, R.A.
▸ Montagu beach house, 'Warren House' Needs Oar Point, Beaulieu, Hants 1956–7
AR Oct 1957 pp.255–8

Casson, Sir Hugh & Conder, Neville & Partners (Neville Conder)
▸ Little Court, Belmont School Lane, Hassocks, E. Sussex, 1957–8
Harling 1961 pp.32–3
BofE Sussex p.518

Casson, Sir Hugh
▸ Ashden House for John Sainsbury and Anya Linden, Lympne, Kent, 1964
H&G Dec 1966 pp.46–9
Harling 1968 pp.48–51
BofE W Kent p.395

Castle, Paul
▸ Father's house, nr Padstow, Cornwall, c.1960

Chamberlin, Powell & Bon (Geoffry Powell)
▸ Dr E. Rossdale house, 30a Hendon Avenue, London N2, 1958–9
AD Sept 1958 pp.347–50
AD Nov 1959 pp.451–3
Pidgeon & Crosby 1960 pp.76–9
Nairn 1964 p.165
Harwood 2000 7.52
Listed grade II

Chapman Taylor & Partners (Bobby Chapman)
▸ Elizabeth Kendall and David Mitchell mews house, Kensington, c.1960
Harling 1963 pp.88–9

Chapman Taylor & Partners (P. Quin)
▸ 35 Kinnerton Street SW1, 1975
McKean & Jestico 1976 p.84

Charter Building Design Group (Dunham, Peter)
▸ Own house 'Gladley house', Leighton Buzzard, Beds, 1971
McKean 1982 p.144

Charter Building Design Group (Formerly Thompson and Chipperfield)
▸ Japanese Garden house, Cottered, Beds, 1976
ERA May–June 1971 pp.23
Herts 1979 p.38
McKean 1982 p.160

Chick, Eric, with Powell & Moya
▸ The 'Highworth House', prototype 1951, Kingsclere, Hants, 1953

Chrzaszcz, Ludwik
▸ Own house, Camden Town, London NW1
IH Aug 1970 pp.40–3

Churcher, Nev
▸ Own house, 'Jamaica Cottage', Jamaica Place, Gosport, Hants, 1975

Cicalese, Anthony – see entry under Boys Jarvis Partnership

Claxton, Kenneth
▸ Own house 'Millponds Studio', Mill Lane, Steep, Petersfield, Hants, 1960
ABN 23 Dec 1964 pp.1223–5
CL 2 April 1964 p.791
IH May 1972 pp.29–35
Bldg 7 July 1972 pp.55, 60–2

Clayton, Robin
▸ House at Gayton, Wirral
ANW Aug 1966 p.17
▸ Day house Sandiway, Cheshire
ANW Aug 1966 p.17
▸ House at Liverpool
ANW Aug 1966 p.17
Wood Sept 1966 pp.28–9

Clifford, H. Dalton
▸ Cottage at Lindfield, W. Sussex, 1953
Clifford 1957 p.53

Coates, Wells (with Michael Lyell)
▸ House at Thames Ditton, Surrey, 1956
Emanuel 1980 p.157
▸ House at West Wittering, W. Sussex, 1956
Emanuel 1980 p.157

Collymore, Peter
▸ Own house, 3 Highbury Terrace Mews, London N5
AJ 24 May 1972 pp.1139–54
H&G Sept 1973 pp.98–9
McKean & Jestico 1976 pp.79, 81

Colquhoun, Alan and Miller, John
▸ Pillwood (Miller) house, Feock, Cornwall, 1974
Emanuel 1980 p.161

Conran, Terence and Shirley
▸ Own terrace house, nr Regent's Park, London NW1, c.1960
Hope 1963 pp.109–11

Cook, Alan
▸ Bel-Air, Lower Street, Horning, Norfolk, 1956

Cowell, Drewitt and Wheatley
▸ Headmaster's house, Penzance, Cornwall, 1949
Clifford 1957 p.54

Cowan, Ralph
▸ Doctor's house in Edinburgh
Penn 1954 p.41

Craig, Stirling & Margaret
▸ The Close, Rectory Lane, Stevenage 1961
Nairn 1964 p.96
▸ Lane House, Barnet Road, Arkley, Herts, 1961
▸ Own house, 3A Hampstead Road, Highgate, 1967–8

Crane, Frazer
▸ House for George Best, Bramhall, Manchester

Croghan, David
▸ House, Cambridge
ERA May/June 1971 pp.24–5

Cubitt, James, and Partners (Stefan Buzas)
▸ House at 57 Ham Street, Ham Common, Surrey, 1952–4
▸ Own house, 59 Ham Street, Ham Common, Surrey, 1952–4
ABN 21 Oct 1954
AR Dec 1954 pp.363–7
H&G Jan 1955 p.43
H&G Mar 1955 pp.66–9
Walter 1955/7 pp.46–9

Cubitt, James & Partners (Fello Atkinson & Brenda Walker)
▸ Goddard house, 22 Avenue Road, Leicester 1953–5 and added garden room, 1958
AR Dec 1955 pp.368–71
CL 5 Dec 1957 pp.1218–19
Daily Mail Ideal Home Book 1957
H&G Dec 1955 pp.68–74
Clifford 1957 pp.55–7
Harling 1961 pp.46–7
Perspectives Jan 1995
Harwood 2000 2.12
Listed grade II

Cubitt, James & Partners
▸ Dr Gordon Walker house, Oulton Broad, Suffolk
H&G June 1956 pp.64–7
Harling 1961 pp.52–3

Cullinan, Edward
▸ Horder House, Ashford Chase, Petersfield, Hants, 1960
Whiting 1964 pp.76–78
Powell 1995 pp.56–7
▸ Knox house I, New Maltings, Nayland, Suffolk, 1964
AR Mar 1971 pp.188–90

- Own house, 62 Camden Mews, London NW1, 1965
  McKean & Jestico 1976 p.42
  'Edward Cullinan Architects' 1984
  Newton 1992
  Jones & Woodward 1992 p.62
  Newton 1992 pp.44–49
  Powell 1995 pp.60–3
- Kawecki house, Bartholomew Villas, London NW5, 1965
  Powell 1995
- Garret house, Greenholm Road, London SE9, 1966
  Emanuel 1980 p.183
- House and barns, Little London Farm, Oakley, Aylesbury, Bucks, 1968
  Emanuel 1980 p.183
- Law house, Hants, 1966–8
  Powell 1995
- Knox house II, New Maltings, Nayland, Suffolk, 1969
  Emanuel 1980 p.183

Curtis, Edward J.W.

- Own Solar House at Rickmansworth, Herts, 1957–8
  AD 1957 pp.15–17
  ABN Jan 1957 pp.24–31
  BofE Herts p.281

Curtis, Edward (Comprehensive Design Group)

- House for Dr Mettam, Blyth, Nottingham
  ABN 12 Aug 1964 pp.301–4

Cybulski, Jan

- Jack Lunn house, Oakwood, Leeds, 1958
  Br 22 Mar 1959 pp.539–41

Dannatt, Trevor

- Richard Church house (conversion from oast-houses begun by F.L. Marcus, 1939), nr Goudhurst, Kent, 1952
  Dannatt 1972 p.11
  Clifford & Enthoven 1954 pp.70–1
- Prof. Peter Laslett house, 3 Clarkson Road, Cambridge, 1958–9
  H&G 1959 pp.90–1
  Pidgeon & Crosby 1960 pp.98–101
  Whiting 1964 pp.154–7
  Booth & Taylor 1970 p.189
  Dannatt 1972 pp.25–7
  McKean 1982 p.19
- Dobbs house, 3 Oakhill Way, London NW3, 1958
  Dannatt 1972 p.24
  BofE London IV p.230
- Plante house, between 5 & 6 Templewood Avenue, London NW3, 1960–1
  Harling 1961 pp.99–101
  Hope 1963 pp.86–9
  Lambert 1963 p.69
  Dannatt 1972 pp.28–9
  BofE London IV p.232
- Lord Balniel house 'Pitcorthie House', Colinsburgh, Fife, 1966
  Harling 1968 pp.68–71
  CL 30 May 1968
  Dannatt 1972 pp.72–5

Darbourne and Darke

- House at Clapham, London, 1964
  DBZ Nov 1966 p.939

Darke, Geoffrey

- House at 25 Montpelier Row, Twickenham, Middlesex, 1969
  McKean & Jestico 1976 p.67

Dartford, James

- H. Sommer house, Somerset Rd, Merton, Wimbledon, London
  ABN 22 Sept 1965 pp.545–8

Dearden, D.G.

- Own house, Weston Road, Wilmslow, Cheshire, 1965
  Sharp, Manchester, p.126

Dennys, John, for Farrington, Dennys, Fisher

- Eaton Hall, Cheshire, for 5th Duke of Westminster, 1971–3 (demolished)
  AR May 1975, pp.293–8
  Robinson 1984 pp.136, 208

Devereux & Davies

- House at New Road, Esher, Surrey, 1955

Diamond, Redfern & Ptrs

- Two houses (one for Alan Redfern, one for L. Kansas) Mapperley Park, Nottingham, c.1964
  ABN 27 Apr 1966 pp.755–6
  AR Dec 1964 pp.736–40
  AEM June–July 1966 p.23

Digby, Jack

- Own house 'Matsudana', Hall Park, Great Barton, Suffolk, 1966
  McKean 1982 p.102

Dinerman, Davison and Hillman

- F.J. Salfield house 'Fleet House', Admiral's Walk, London NW3, 1956
  Hope 1963 pp.75–82

Dingle

- Dawes House at Kingswear, Devon, 1958

Dockray, Brian (of Shaw, Dockray and Dent)

- House at Kendal, Cumbria
  IH Nov 1965 pp.54–5

Dore and Wurr (T.P and N.J. Wurr)

- Own house, Pinner, Middlesex, 1953–4
  Bldg 10 April 1970
  Clifford 1957 p.128

Dowson, Sir Philip – see entries under Arup Associates

Dransfield, Lydia

- House in Wimbledon, London, c.1953
  Penn 1954 pp.55, 69
  Newton 1992 pp.8–13

Dredge, Derek, and Tebbutt, John

- House for Mr Day, Tewin, Herts
  ERA May–June 1971 p.18

Drew, Jane

- High Acre, Hyver Hill, Barnet, 1960
  BofE London IV p.182

Drury, Brian

- House for Paul Gerrard, West Wickham, Kent
  ABN 2 Sept 1964 pp.442–5

Dry, David, Halasz, K. & Associates

- Hoellering house 'Upton Wood Farm', Fulmer, Bucks, 1962
  Whiting 1964 pp.79–83
- House for Marcus Sewell and John Haryett, Popesgrove, Twickenham
  ABN 14 Sept 1966 pp.471–2

Duckett, Rix and Scott

- House at Sonning-on-Thames, Berks, 1955
  Clifford 1957 pp.58–9
- House at Tunbridge Wells, Kent, 1955
  Clifford 1957 p.60

Dunham, Peter

- Additions to own house, Luton, Beds, c.1951–2
  H&G November 1952 pp.56–7

Dunham, Widdup & Harrison

- F. Macfarlane Widdup house, Dunstable, Beds, 1952
  H&G May 1954 pp.76–7, 128
  Penn 1954 p.129
  Walter 1955/7 pp.52–3

Dunham, Widdup & Harrison (R.S. Williamson)

- Own house, Redbourn, Herts, 1950
  Walter 1955/7 p.106

Dunham, Peter – see also entry under Charter Building Design

Dykes Bower, Stephen

- St Vedast's Rectory, 4 Foster Lane, London EC1, 1959
  CL 2 June 1960
  Harwood 2000 8.22
  Listed grade II

Echenique, Marcial

- House at 214 Chesterton Road, Cambridge, 1972
  BM Jan 1978 pp.20–22
  McKean 1982 p.42

Erith, Raymond

- House at Jupes Hill, Dedham, Essex, 1948–9
  Archer 1985 pp.126–7
- 15–19 Aubrey Walk, Kensington 1951–2
  Archer 1985 pp.128–30
  Harwood 2000 7.24
  Listed Grade II
- Peter Marsh cottage 'Lower Lufkins', Bargate Lane, Dedham, Essex, 1952–3
  Archer 1985 p.134
- Farm cottage at Great Wenham, Suffolk, 1954
  Archer 1985 pp.57, 134
- The Red House, Gandish Road, East Bergholt, Suffolk, 1955
  Archer 1985 pp.58, 123
- John Buxton house 'Morley Hall', Wareside, Herts, 1955–7
  Archer 1985 pp.76–8
- Elizabeth Watt house 'The Pediment', Aynho, Northants, 1956–7
  Archer 1985 pp.141–4
  Harwood 2000 2.18
  Listed grade II
- The Mount, Lamb Corner, Dedham, Essex, 1963
  Archer 1985 pp.58, 134
- Additions to Bentley Farm, Halland, E. Sussex, for Gerald Askew, 1960–1, 1969–71
  CL 13, 20 Sept 1984
  Archer 1985 pp.156–61
  Harwood 2000 6.14
  Listed grade II
- Provost's Lodgings, Queen's College, Queen's Lane, Oxford, 1958–60
  CL 7 July 1960 pp.34–6
  Archer 1985 pp.62–7, 145
  Harwood 2000 5.14
  Listed grade II
- 'The Folly', Gatley Park, Leinthall Earls, Hereford & Worcs, 1961–3; and addition 1973–6
  H&G Feb 1966 pp.32–5
  Archer 1985 pp.128–33, 161
  Harwood 2000 2.54
  Listed grade II
- Gooch house, Wivenhoe New Park, Wivenhoe, Colchester, Essex, 1962–4
  CL 22 July 1965 p.218
  McKean 1982 p.120
  Archer 1985 pp.171–3
- Willow House and Lawrence House, Walsham-le-Willows, Suffolk, 1967–8
  Archer 1985 pp.187–8
- Reginald Duthy house 'Joscelyns', Little Horkesley, Essex, 1967–70
  Archer 1985 p.194
- Pound House, Gaston Street, East Bergholt, Suffolk, 1970
  Archer 1985 pp.58, 204

Erith, Raymond, and Terry, Quinlan

- Kingswalden Bury House, Hitchen, Herts, 1970–2
  AJ 3 May 1972 p.953
  Bldg 5 May 1972 p.61
  CL 27 Sept 1973 pp.858–61 & 4 Oct 1973 pp.970–4
  Terry, Quinlan, Kingswalden Notes MCMLXX, Pentagram Papers 16, n.d.
  Herts 1979 p.47
  McKean 1982 p.165

Fairlie, Reginald

- Baro House, Gifford, E. Lothian, 1939, completed 1955
  Robinson 1984 p.200
  BoS Lothian p.210

Farquharson, Horace, and McMorran, Donald

- McMorran, own house, 1 Falkland Grove, Dorking, Surrey, *Penn 1954, frontispiece*

Ffloydd, John

▸ Russell house, Folkestone, Kent
ABN 22 Sept 1965 pp.549–52

Fielden & Mawson

▸ House and office, 71a Cathedral
Close, Norwich, 1955
AJ 17 Jan 1973 p.148
McKean 1982 p.72

Finch, Richard

▸ House at West Mersea, 1955

Findlay, John (of K.D. Homes)

▸ House and Garden A-Frame cottage,
for Ideal Home Exhibition, c.1962
Harling 1963 pp.98–9

Fitzherbert-Brockholes, Fulke

▸ Leagram Hall, Lancashire, for Charles
Weld-Blundell, c.1960
Robinson 1984 p.216

▸ Claughton Hall, Garstang,
Lancashire, for Michael Fitzherbert-
Brockholes, 1965
Robinson 1984 p.205

Fletcher, Ross and Hickling

▸ House at Thorner, Leeds
YA Mar–Apr 1969 pp.102–3

Fletcher-Watson, James

▸ Warham House, Holt, Norfolk, 1957

▸ House at Cley, Norfolk, 1956
Br 1 Feb 1957

▸ Bishop's House, Norwich, 1959
BofE, Norfolk I 1999 p.221

▸ East Carleton Manor, Norfolk, for
Colin Chapman, 1964
Robinson 1984 pp.116, 208

▸ Watlington Hall, Norfolk, 1965
Robinson 1984 pp.114, 231

Flinder, Alexander

▸ 41 Frognal, London NW3, 1966–8
BofE London IV p.228–9

Foggo, Peter & Thomas, David

▸ Bob Swash House, 44 Lonsdale
Square, London N1, 1957

▸ George Scott house 'Sorrell House',
Bosham Hoe, Chichester, W. Sussex,
1960
BD 12 Aug 1994
Harwood 2000 6.12
Listed grade II*

▸ Three houses, 1–3 Manor Way,
Holyport, Bray, Bucks, 1964

▸ Forrester house, Murray Road,
Wimbledon, SW19, c.1963

▸ Three houses at 31B St Mary's Road,
Wimbledon, SW19

▸ Judge Smalley house, Blackheath

▸ Douglas Foggo house, Buxton,
Derbyshire, 1967

▸ 78 Cambridge Street, (architects' own
maisonnettes plus 2 flats) London
SW1, 1968–9
BofE London I (1973), p.636

Ford, J.A.

▸ House at Wormley Hill, nr
Godalming, Surrey, 1955
Clifford 1957 p.66

Foulkes, S. Colwyn

▸ Brynhyryd Villa, Denbigh, 1956
BoW Clwyd p.154

▸ Own house, 'Moryn', 27 Cayley
Promenade, Llandrillo-yn-Rhos,
Clwyd, c.1960
BoW Clwyd p.195

▸ 23 Ebberston Road West, Llandrillo-
yn-Rhos, Clwyd, 1960–1
BoW Clwyd p.195

Fry, Maxwell, and Drew, Jane

▸ Studio at Rowfant, E. Sussex, c.1960
Harling 1961 pp.120–1

Fryman, John G.

▸ Scott Anderson house, 'Fram', Knotty
Green, Beaconsfield, Bucks, 1961–62
Whiting 1964 pp.16–21
AR Sept 1964 pp.171–3
ABN 10 Feb 1965

**Fryman, John G.
(assisted by F.L. Hawes)**

▸ Robin Pitman house, Spinfield Lane,
Marlow, Bucks
Whiting 1964 pp.130–134

Gardiner, Stephen

▸ 55 Fitzroy Park, London N6, 1952
AJ 25 Sept 1952
Penn 1954 p.154

▸ House at Blackheath Park, London
SE3, 1958
H&G Dec 1958
Pidgeon & Crosby 1960 pp.92–3
Harling 1961 pp.104–5

▸ Col. Walker house, Faringdon, Oxon,
1964
BD 25 Jan 1974, pp.15–6

▸ House for a teacher, Redhill, Surrey,
1964

▸ Capt. Villiers house, Banbury Road,
Oxford, 1965

**Gardiner, Stephen, & Knight,
Christopher**

▸ Stratton Park, Micheldever, Hants,
1964–5
(retaining portico by George Dance)
AR March 1965 pp.182–5

**Garnett, Cloughley,
Blakesmore & Associates**

▸ Hillside house for chairman of BNI,
Chiltern, Bucks
H&G Feb 1970, pp.48–53

**Garnett, Cloughley,
Blakemore & Associates
(Anthony Cloughley)**

▸ House at Avington Park, Hants
H&G Dec–Jan 1972–3 pp.72–3

**Garnett & Cloughley
(Patrick Garnett)**

▸ Garnett house, 11 Clayton Drive,
Prestatyn, Clwyd, 1962
BoW Clwyd p.419

▸ New House, Maes-y-Don Avenue,
Rhyl, Clwyd, 1961
BoW Clwyd p.434

▸ Mrs Garnett house, 7 The Boulevard,
Rhyl, Clwyd, 1960
BoW Clwyd p.434

▸ Patrick Garnett house, 1 The
Boulevard, Rhyl, Clwyd, 1962
BoW Clwyd p.434

**Garnett, Cloughley, Blakemore
& Associates**

▸ Garnett house, 150 Rhuddlan Road,
Rhyl, Clwyd, 1965–6
BoW Clwyd p.434

**Gasson, Barry, and Meunier,
John**

▸ Wendon House, 39 New Road,
Barton, Cambs, 1965
AD Oct 1967 pp.480
IH Oct 1966 pp.66–9
B&W Dec 1970 pp.440–1
Booth & Taylor 1970 pp.197–8
Park 1971, pp.36–9
McKean 1982 p.42

▸ Edington house, Little Eversden,
Cambs, 1974–5
McKean 1982 p.45

**Gauldie, Hardie, Wright &
Needham**

▸ 'Tayside', Invergowrie, Dundee, 1952
Penn 1954 pp.46, 70
McKean & Walker 1984 pp.130–1

Gazzard, R.A.J.

▸ Own house, Wimbledon, London,
1950
Clifford 1957 p.68

Geden, Roy

▸ Mistral, Kenilworth Road, Coventry,
1968

Gibberd, Sir Frederick

▸ Own house, Marsh Lane, Harlow,
Essex (adaptation of 1907 bungalow),
1962

**Gibberd, Vernon
(Vernon Gibberd Assoc)**

▸ House at Kingston, Surrey
AR Aug 1971 pp.73–5

Gibbs, Peter

▸ 'Mudbrook', Ashdown Forest, Sussex
ABN 14 June 1967 pp.1031–6
DBZ Apr 1969 pp.607–10

Gibson, Alexander

▸ House at Chorley Wood, Herts, 1952
Walter 1955/7 p.65

▸ House at 5 Cannon Lane, London
NW3, 1954–5
AD Dec 1953
AR Aug 1955 pp.85–8
H&G Nov 1955 pp.66–9
Harling 1961 pp.108–9

Gibson, Richard

▸ House at 20 Murray Mews, London
NW1, 1965
AR Aug 1968 pp.115–6
Jones & Woodward 1992 pp.61–2

Gilbert & Hobson

▸ Haddock & McDowell beach house
'Chert', Ventnor, IoW, 1967
NT Spring 2000 no.89, pp.52–4

**Gilbert and Partners
(Jack Godfrey Gilbert)**

▸ Cohen house, Golf Club Drive/
Coombe Hill Drive, New Malden,
Surrey
[TB] Br 4 June 1965 pp.1215–6

Gill, J.C.

▸ Post Knot, Bowness, Cumbria
ANW Dec 63–Jan 64 p.45

Goalen, Martin

▸ 30 College Lane, London NW5
BofE Lodon IV p.395

Goldfinger, Ernö

▸ Two houses incl. Fletcher house,
Henley-in-Arden, Warwickshire,
1947–9
AR 1948 p.182
AJ 17 Aug 1950 pp.162–4
Emanuel 1980 p.295
Dunnett & Stamp 1983 p.77

▸ Caretaker's house, Brandlehow Road
School, London SW15, for LCC, 1951
Walter 1955/7 p.99

▸ House on dairy farm, Turville, Bucks
ABN 4 Feb 1954
AD April 1954
Dunnett & Stamp 1983 p.85

▸ Four staff houses for John Boyce of
Wellesley House School, 151–3 (odd)
Ramsgate Road, Broadstairs, Kent,
1952–3
AD Nov 1953, pp.313–4
AD Dec 1954
Penn 1954 pp.52–3
Dunnett & Stamp 1983 p.86

▸ House at High Street, Old Amersham,
Bucks, c.1956
AD Oct 1957
H&G May 1958
Harling 1961 pp.43–5
Dunnett & Stamp 1983 p.86

▸ Player house 'Lime Tree House',
Coombe Hill, Kingston-upon-
Thames, Surrey, 1961–2
(demolished 1995)
BM Dec 1964
Emanuel 1980 p.295
Dunnett & Stamp 1983 pp.88, 114

▸ Dr Hans Motz house, 16 Bedford
Street, Oxford, 1964
Emanuel 1980 p.295
Dunnett & Stamp 1983 pp.88, 114

▸ Perry House, 'Benjamin's Mount',
Westwood Road, Windlesham,
Surrey, 1967–9
Dunnett & Stamp 1983, pp.124–5
Harwood 2000 6.38
Listed Grade II*

Gollins, Frank, Melvin, James, Ward, Edmund & Partners
▸ House at Campden Hill, London w8
AR Aug 1971 pp.90–3

Goodair, A.G.
▸ House in Pembroke Road, Old Portsmouth, Hants, 1951–2

Gooday, Leslie and Noble, Wycliffe
▸ Gooday house, East Sheen, London sw14, c.1952
H&G Dec 1953 pp.54–7, 93

Gooday, Leslie
▸ House at Reigate, Surrey, 1953
Clifford 1957 p.74
▸ 'Serenity', St George's Hill, Weybridge, Surrey, 1958
CL 4 Sept 1958 pp.484–5
▸ Gooday house 'Long Wall', Golf Club Road, Weybridge, Surrey 1964–8
IH Sept 1968 pp.30–4
Park 1971 pp.102–7
Harwood 2000 6.36
Listed grade II
▸ Wheatcroft, Forest Drive, Kingswood, Kingston upon Thames, Surrey, 1958
BofE Surrey p.337
▸ Winder house, Ham Common, Kingston upon Thames, Surrey
H&G July–Aug 1969 pp.52–5

Goodhart-Rendel, H.S. & Partners
▸ Adeane house, 1 Dean Trench Street, London sw1
Powers 1987, p.25
Harwood 2000 8.8
Listed Grade II
▸ St John the Divine Vicarage (former convent), 92 Vassall Road, & former caretaker's cottage, 96 Vassall Road, Kennington, London sw9, 1952–5
Powers 1987 p.60
Harwood 2000 9.14
Listed Grade II

Gordon, Rodney
▸ Own house, 'Turnpoint', Onslow Road, Burwood Park, Walton-on-Thames, Surrey, 1961–2
Harwood 2000 6.20
Listed Grade II
▸ Iredale house 'Woodhouse', Onslow Road, Burwood Park, Walton-on-Thames, Surrey, 1965–6
Wood July 1968 pp.22–3
Space (The Guardian) 3 Feb 2000 pp.12–15

Gosschalk, John
▸ House at Chenies Avenue, Little Chalfont, Bucks
Bldg 10 June 1966 pp.99–101

Gotelee, Alan
▸ Wasing Place, Berkshire, for Sir William Mount, Bt, 1957
Robinson 1984 p.231

Gowan, James – see also entries under Stirling & Gowan

Gowan, James (with Frank Newby)
▸ Schreiber house, West Heath Road, London NW3, 1963–4
AJ 14 July 1965, pp.103–114
AD 1965, pp.294–308
Park 1971 pp.44–49
Emanuel 1980 p.302
Gowan 1994
Harwood 2000 7.74
Listed Grade II

Gowan, James
▸ 'Greenbank House' for Schreiber family, 8 Greenbank, Eaton Road, Chester, 1964
Emanuel 1980 p.302
Gowan 1994 pp.112–3

Graham, Harry
▸ Brockenhurst Park, Hants, for the Hon Denis & Mrs Berry, 1965
CL 31 Aug 1967
Robinson 1984 p.203

Grahame MacDougall, Leslie
▸ Ulva House, Ulva, Argyllshire, for Edith, Lady Congleton, c.1953
Robinson 1984 p.230
▸ Connel, Argyllshire, for the Captain of Dunstaffnage
Robinson 1984 p.205

Gray, David
▸ Fishery Research Officer's house, Lowestoft, 1956–8 (overclad) (House & Garden House of the Year 1959)
Harling 1961 pp.40–2

Greaves, Walter
▸ O'Keefe house, Corner Green, Blackheath (with Peter Moro), 1960
▸ Leslie Bilsby house, off Morden Road, Blackheath, 1966
▸ Morris Shapira house, Leycroft Close, Canterbury, Kent, (with Ian Morton-Wright), 1967
▸ Greaves house ('Severals'), Runcton Lane, Runcton, Chichester, W. Sussex, 1981

Green, Cedric
▸ 'Delta' (an A-frame house), Charsfield, Suffolk, 1974
McKean 1982 p.100

Greenwood, Sydney, and Michell, Howard N.
▸ House at Totteridge Lane, London N20, 1954
Walter 1955/7 pp.20–1

Griffiths, Stephen
▸ House at East Molesey, Surrey
IH Nov 1965 pp.56–7

Grimshaw, Anthony J.
▸ Bell house, Crossdale Drive, Parbold, nr Wigan, Lancs, 1961
▸ Black house, Park Close, Lancaster Lane, Parbold, nr Wigan, Lancs 1963
AR Sept 1963 pp.188–91
▸ Ellison house, Hindley Mill Lane, nr Wigan, Lancs 1962
AR Sept 1963 pp.188–91
▸ Naylor house, 7A Laurel Grove, Ashton-in-Makerfield, nr Wigan, Lancs 1963
▸ Boardman house, 'Redwood', Winchester Avenue, Ashton-in-Makerfield, nr Wigan, Lancs, 1962
▸ Parr house, Long Lane, Aughton, nr Ormskirk, Lancs, 1963
▸ Grindrod house, 'Lorien', Red Rock Lane, Haigh, nr Wigan, Lancs 1964
▸ Cunningham house, 10 Crawford Avenue, Aldington, Lancs, 1967
▸ Grindrod house, 'Cerin Amroth', Beechfield Road, Alderley Edge, Cheshire, 1972

Grundy and Harmer
▸ Newman house, Stoughton Drive South, Oadby, Leicester
AEM 1970 no.30 p.39

Guest, Patric
▸ Robert Welch house, 'The White House', Alveston, Warwickshire, 1962
D. Hickman Shell Guide
▸ David Mellor house, 1 Park Lane, Sheffield, 1959–60

Gwynne, Patrick
▸ Leslie Bilsby house, Blackheath Park, London SE3, 1949 (demolished 1967)
IH Nov 1971 pp.47–51
Gwynne nd
▸ Jack Hawkins house, Bournemouth, 1958
Br 18 Mar 1960 pp.545–7
Gwynne nd
▸ Otto Edler house 'The Firs', 24 Spaniard's End, London NW3, 1958
Br 19 Feb 1960 pp.356–9
Gwynne nd
Harwood 2000 7.46
Listed Grade II
▸ Dr A. Salmon house 'Past Field', 9 Rotherfield Road, Henley-on-Thames, Oxon, 1959–60; and additions, c.1970
Whiting 1964 pp.118–22
Gwynne nd
Harwood 2000 5.24
Listed Grade II
▸ Four houses 'Fairoaks', 'Mulberry', 'Woodlands' and 'Junipers' (demolished), Coombe Hill Road, Kingston upon Thames, Surrey, 1959
AR June 1961
Hope 1963 pp.83–5
Park 1971 p.105
▸ Bruh house, 4 Beechworth Close, London NW3, 1961
Gwynne nd
Harwood 2000 7.58
Listed Grade II
▸ Gerald Bentall house, Witley Park, Godalming, Surrey, 1961–3
Gwynne nd
▸ Hornung house, 3 Beechworth Close, London NW3, 1963
Gwynne nd
▸ Shaw house, Wentworth Estate, Sunningdale, Surrey, 1965 (demolished c.1993)
IH Oct 1966 p.71
Gwynne nd
▸ Leslie Bilsby house, 10 Blackheath Park, London SE3, 1969
Gwynne nd
McKean & Jestico 1976 p.78
Listed Grade II

Haddon, Tony
▸ House in Kettering, Northamptonshire
AEM Nov–Dec 1969

Haire, David Anthony
▸ Own house, 30 Caldy Road, West Kirby, Cheshire, 1967

Hancock & Swannell
▸ 'Freechase', Warninglid, Sussex, for Sir Gawaine Baillie Bt 1975
AR May 1977 pp.314–7
Robinson 1984 p.152, 209

Harbinson, L.R.
▸ Longbourne, Totteridge, Barnet, c.1973
BofE London IV p.190

Hare and Pert
▸ K.G. Pert house, Nettlestead, Suffolk
ABN 12 Aug 1964 pp.305–8

Harding, D.E.
▸ 'Shollond Hill', Nacton, Suffolk, 1955
BofE Suffolk p.370

Harris, John (with Stuart Davis)
▸ Ian and Dorothy Warren house, Swain's Wood, Henley, Chilterns
Bldg 16 Feb 1968 pp.153–6
Harling 1968 pp.20–3

Harris, Seymour & Partners
▸ Seymour Harris house, 'Tukal', Beaulieu, Hants, 1970
Aslet & Powers, 1985, p.260

Hartry, Edward & Teresa
▸ House at Ivy Lane, Maybury, Woking, Surrey, 1960
Whiting 1964 pp.29–33

Hartry, Grover & Halter
▸ 'Willow Loft', Hurley, Berks, 1962
Whiting 1964 pp.34–37

Hartshorn, A.G.J., & Swain, Henry T.
▸ House at Exeter, Devon
Penn 1954 pp.57, 113

Harvey, Robert, of Yorke, Harper & Harvey

▸ K.B.L. Bailey house at Tanworth-in-Arden, Warwickshire, 1954
ABN 13 Nov 1957 p.631

▸ Harvey house, 112 Kenilworth Road, Coventry, 1956–7

▸ 114 Kenilworth Road, Coventry, 1956–7

▸ Own house, Ilmington, Warwickshire, 1957

▸ House in Frog Lane, Ilmington, Warwickshire, 1959

▸ The Round House, Ilmington, Warwickshire, 1962

▸ 9 Gibbet Hill Road, Coventry, 1963

▸ Tall Trees, Tredington, Warwickshire, 1963

▸ R.M. Wilson house, 'South Winds', Cryfield Grange Road, Coventry, 1965–6
G. Lewison & R. Billingham, Coventry: New Architecture 1969 pp.95–7

▸ Povey house, Barford, Warwickshire, 1966–9

Haward, Birkin

▸ Haward house, 'The Spinney', 108 Westerfield Road, Ipswich, Suffolk, 1960

▸ 'The Nook', Primrose Alley, South Green, Southwold, Suffolk, 1971
McKean 1982 p.109

Heal, Victor

▸ Newsells Park, Hertfordshire, for Sir Humphrey de Trafford, Bt, 1954
Robinson 1954 pp.220–1

Henson, Colonel A.F.

▸ Own house, Farthingstone, Northants
Bldg 10 Feb 1967 pp.85–7

Hesketh, Colonel Roger Fleetwood

▸ Alterations to Meols Hall, Churchtown, Southport, Lancs, 1960–4
CL 25 January, 1 & 8 February 1973
Robinson 1984
Harwood 2000 1.52
Listed Grade II*

Higgins, Ney and Partners

▸ 'Heathbrow', Spaniards End, London NW3, 1961
CL 9 May 1963 pp.1052–3
Harling 1961 pp.36–7

▸ 8A Fitzroy Park, London N6
AJ 4 April 1973 pp.794–810
Harwood 2000 7.76
Listed Grade II

Hill, Oliver

▸ Cock Rock, Croyde, Barnstaple, Devon, (rebuilding after fire) 1953–4
CL 15 May 1958 pp.1080–2

▸ Golodetz house, 'The Pavilion', Coombe Hill Road, Kingston upon Thames, Surrey, 1958–61
CL 28 Dec 1961, pp.1636–8
H&G Sept 1965 pp.60–3
Harwood 2000 9.42
Listed Grade II

▸ Morris-Keating house, Long Newnton Priory, Glos., 1963–6
CL 25 Sept 1969 pp.750–2
Powers 1987 p.54

Hill, R. Towning

▸ House at Draycott, nr Cheddar, Somerset, 1955–7
Clifford 1957 pp.72–3
Harling 1961 pp.60–1

▸ House nr Long Ashton, Bristol
Harling 1961 pp.58–9

Hinton, Denys

▸ Tibor Reich house, 23 Avenue Road, Stratford-on-Avon, Warwickshire
CL 18 Sept 1958 pp.609–10

Hodgkinson, Patrick

▸ Adrian house, Burrell's Field, Cambridge, 1964 (demolished c.1994)
Stephen 1965, pp.66–70

Holister, Darnton

▸ Own house 'White Walls', opp. church, Kingston, Cambs, 1965
Booth & Taylor 1970 pp.200–1
McKean 1982 p.51

Holroyd, Geoffrey & June

▸ House at High Wray, Eccleshall, Yorkshire, 1958
AD June 1958 p.245

▸ House at Eccleshall, Sheffield, 1958
AR April 1958 p.10

Hope, Beryl

▸ House at Pirbright, Surrey
AR Dec 1967 pp.461–3

Hopkins, Michael & Patty

▸ Own house, 49a Downshire Hill, London NW3, 1975
Jones & Woodward 1992 p.53
Newton 1992 pp.94–99

Horsfall, G.F.

▸ House at Little Aston Park, Staffs, 1955

Horden, Richard

▸ Horden House (for parents) 'Boat House', Branscombe Park, Poole, Dorset, 1975

Horton, Earle & Associates

▸ Own house, 16a Spencer Hill, London SW19, 1969
McKean & Jestico 1976 p.64

Housden, Brian

▸ Own house, 78 South Hill Park, London NW3, 1968
Jones & Woodward 1982 p.52

Howard, Peter

▸ Dr Sanctuary house, Laleham, Surrey
ABN 13 Oct 1965 pp.685–8

Howard, Robert, and Pank, Philip

▸ Philip Pank house, Torriano Cottages, London NW5
AR Jan 1967 p.38
AJ 2 Sept 1970 pp.523–6
Newton 1992 pp.66–71

▸ Harvey Unna house, 38 Millfield Lane, London N6, 1969
AR Mar 1971 pp.183–7
McKean & Jestico 1976 p.76

Howard-Radley, M.

▸ 7–7B Cresswell Place, London SW10, 1969
BofE London III p.550

Howell, William & Gillian

▸ Trestrail house 'Broadribb Cottage', Wisborough Green, W. Sussex, 1954–5
H&G June 1955 pp.52–3
AD June 1955
Clifford 1957 pp.80–1

Howell, William, & Amis, Stanley

▸ Houses at 80–90 (even) South Hill Park, London NW3, 1955
AR Nov 1956, pp.290–5
AD Dec 1956 pp.402–6
H&G Feb 1957 pp.48–53
Harling 1961 pp.86–9
Lambert 1963 p.70
Cantacuzino 1981 pp.50–1
Newton 1992 pp.14–19
Jones & Woodward 1992 p.51

Howell, Killick, Partridge and Amis (W.G. Howell)

▸ Little Ruffo, Trebarwith Strand, Cornwall, 1958–9
Harling 1963 pp.92–3
Cantacuzino 1981, p.57

Howell, Killick, Partridge and Amis

▸ Dr John Woodhall house at St Paul's Cray, Kent, 1951–3
AD Jan 1955
H&G Jan 1955 p.43

▸ North house 'Ravensbourne', Keston Common, Bromley, Kent, 1958–60 (demolished 1992)
AR Oct 1964 pp.288
Cantacuzino 1981 pp.54–5

▸ Little Wakestone, Sussex (addition), 1963–65
Whiting 1964 pp.98–103

▸ Houses at Warwick University for visiting mathematicians, 1968–70 (RIBA regional award 1970)
RIBAJ July 1970 p.298
AWM No.4 Feb 1971 pp.11, 13, 15
Emanuel 1980 p.380

Hughes, Basil

▸ Snaigow, Dunkeld, Perthshire, for 7th Earl Cadogan, 1960–1
Robinson 1984 p.226

Hughes, J. Quentin

▸ House at Noctorum Lane, Ha'pennyfield, Bidston, Cheshire, 1959–60
BofE Cheshire

Hunter, James

▸ Mann House, Woolton, Liverpool
ANW Aug 1966 p.16

Ingham, Keith – see entry under Building Design Partnership

Insall, Donald

▸ Broad Oak, Carmarthen, for Viscount Emlyn, 1960
Robinson 1984 p.203

▸ Ashford Water, Fordingbridge, Hants, 1961
Robinson 1984 p.199

Isaacson, L.R.

▸ Three houses, Furlong Road N7, 1974
McKean & Jestico 1976 p.79

Jaggard, Anthony (of John Stark & Partners, Dorchester)

▸ Lulworth Castle, Dorset, for Sir Joseph Weld, 1975
Robinson 1984 p.218

▸ Kesworth House, Dorset, for Harry Clark, 1979
Robinson pp.213–4

James and Bywaters (Peter Boston)

▸ Elisabeth Vellacott studio house, 4 Langley Way, Hemingford Grey, Cambs, 1959
H&G April 1962 pp.80–1
Harling 1963 pp.90–1

▸ D.P. Forbes Irving house, 48b Netherhall Gardens, London NW3, c.1962
Hope 1963 pp.38–43

James and Bywaters

▸ Terrace houses, 31–7 Rudall Crescent, London NW3, c.1962
Hope 1963 pp.26–9

Jebb, Philip

▸ 12–14 Cheyne Walk, London SW3, 1970

Jefferson & Partners

▸ Ellis House, Inglewood Avenue, Huddersfield, W. Yorkshire, 1962
Whiting 1964 pp.73–75

Jellicoe, Ballantine & Coleridge

▸ 17 West Heath Avenue, London NW3, c.1960
BofE London IV p.138

Jenkins, David

▸ House on wheels, Brentwood, Essex, 1955

▸ House at Brentwood, Essex, 1955
AJ 28 Aug 1952
AJ 19 March 1953

**Jepson, Michael
(of H.N. Jepson & Partners)**
- 7 Leighton Close, Coventry, 1959
Coventry New Architecture 1969, p.81
BB Dec 1963 p.7

Johnson, Francis
- Sir Thomas Ferens house
'Sunderlandwick Hall', Great
Driffield, E. Yorkshire, 1962–4
CL 11 Oct 1984 pp.1008–11
Robinson 1984
Harwood 2000 1.60
Listed Grade II
- David Brotherton house, Whitwell,
N. Yorkshire, 1966
CL 11 Oct 1984 p.1011

Johnson, Nicholas
- Llangoed, Breconshire, for the
Chichester family, 1977–8
Robinson 1984 p.216
- Llanstephan House, Radnorshire,
for Hon Hugo Phillips, 1974–6
Robinson 1984 p.216

Johnston, Ivan & Partners
- House at No.4, Stokeshay, Bidston,
Cheshire, 1966

Jolley, Robert
- The Ranch, Storey Lane, Parbold,
Lancs 1959

Jones & Dennis (Jennifer Jones)
- Jack & Molly Pritchard House, Angel
Lane, Blythburgh, Suffolk, 1963

Katz, Bronek, and Vaughan, R.
- Shipp house, Sutton, Surrey, 1950
Penn 1954 p.141
Walter 1955/7 p.93

**Katz, Bronek, and Vaughan,
R. & Partners (Roger Balkwill
and John Heath)**
- Fred Kobler house 'Hill House'
(formerly 'Baldwins'), Lingfield Road,
East Grinstead, E. Sussex, 1960–2
Whiting 1964 pp.22–8

Kaufmann, Gerd & Associates
- House for Mr and Mrs Scheer, 2
Aylmer Close, Stanmore, Middlesex,
1967
IH May 1972 pp.36–9
ID June 1972 pp.406–8
McKean & Jestico 1976 p.78

Kay, Tom
- J.C.R. Bailey house 'Tower House',
Kensington Place (cnr Hillgate
Street), London W8, c.1966
AR Jan 1967 p.38
AR Aug 1968 pp.113–4
H&G Dec–Jan 1969 pp.44–9
Park 1971 pp.23–7
- Own mews house and Studio, 22
Murray Mews, London NW1, 1971–2
AR 1975
McKean & Jestico 1976 p.41
Murray & Trombley 1990 pp.58–9
Jones & Woodward 1992 p.61
Newton 1992 pp.82–7

**Keene, Roger
(Roger Keene Partnership)**
- Keene house, 1 Bates Road Coventry,
1966
Lewison & Billingham 1969 p.72
- Nassington, Northamptonshire
Bldg 1 Sept 1967 pp.85–6

Kennedy, John
- Own house, St Mary-in-the-Marsh,
New Romney, Kent
IH Apr 1973 pp.44–8

Kinnimonth, Sir William
- Moncrieffe, Bridge of Earn,
Perthshire, for Elizabeth Moncrieffe,
1960
Robinson 1984 p.220
- Philiphaugh, Selkirk, for Sir William
Strang-Steel, Bt, 1965
Robinson 1984 p.223

Lamb, Bernard
- Arthur Pearson house, 240 Barnett
Wood Lane, Ashstead, Surrey, 1952
- Chilcott house, 'Highwood',
Munstead Park, Godalming, Surrey,
1960
- Dr Somerfield house, 23 Somers
Road, Reigate, Surrey, c.1963
- Dower house, Bighton House,
Bighton, nr Arlesford, Hants, for Dr
Sargeant, c.1962
- Robin Bluhm house, Lancaster Place,
Kew, c.1967
- Own maisonette addition, 'The
Studio', 34 Emperor's Gate, London
SW7, 1969

**Lasdun, Sir Denys & Partners
(Alexander Redhouse, job
architect)**
- Sir Timothy Sainsbury 'Hill House'
(Thames House), Union Lane,
Headley, Berks, 1970–1
Robinson 1984 p.150

Law & Dunbar-Nasmith
- Major Sir Hew Hamilton-Dalrymple
house, Leuchie, North Berwick, E.
Lothian, 1961
CL 26 Oct 1961 pp.1020–1
IH Nov 1963 pp.126–7
- Lionel de Rothschild house, Upper
Exbury, Hants, 1964–5
AR CXXXIX 1966 pp.295–8
BofE Hants and IoW 1973 p.217
Robinson 1984 pp.145–8, 208

Lawrence, P.H.
- Artist's house at East Molesey, Surrey,
1955–6
Clifford 1957 p.84

Lee, Maurice
- Own house, Digswell, Herts,
(pre 1957)

Lee, Vernon H.
- Own house, Tewin, Herts, 1953–5
Penn 1954 p.129
Walter 1955/7 pp.74–5

Lee Reading and Harrison
- House at Totteridge Lane,
London N20
Bldg 24 Aug 1973 p.51

Leech, Cecil W.
- Own house, 40a Kenilworth Road,
Coventry, 1968
Lewison & Billingham 1969 p.71

**Leigh-Pemberton, Robin
(with H.G. Freemantle)**
- Own house (Rt Hon Lord Kingsdown
K.G., P.C.) 'Torry Hill', Frinsted,
Kent, 1956–8
BofE North Kent p.317
Robinson 1984 pp.187–8

Lever, Jeremy
- Own house, 29 1/2 Lansdowne
Crescent, London W11, 1973
McKean & Jestico 1976 p.30

Lewis, E. Wamsley
- Thatched house at Langton Herring,
Dorset, 1951
Clifford 1957 pp.88–9
- House at Weymouth, Dorset, 1953
(Housing Medal Award 1955)
Clifford 1957 p.90

Levy, Anthony
- Own house, 21 West Heath Avenue,
London NW11, 1961
AJ 8 July 1964 pp.97–8
H&G Feb 1966 pp.36–8

Levy, Ted, & Benjamin, Isaac
- 1a–e Oval Road, London NW1, 1963
BofE London IV p.386
- 36–38 Gayton Road, London NW3,
1969
BofE London IV p.223
- House in Windmill Hill, London
NW3, 1968–70
BofE London IV p.230
- House at Redington Road, London,
1968–70
D-Extrakt Vol.11 Nov 1972

Lorimer & Matthew
- House at Linburn, Midlothian
Penn 1954 pp.21, 81

Lincoln, John
- House at Standish Hospital, Gloucs.
ABN 30 June 1965 pp.1213–6

Lingard and Williams
- Doctor's house at Brynciencyn,
Anglesey, 1953–4
Clifford 1957 pp.86–7

Llewelyn-Davies, Richard
- House at Mayford, Surrey, 1955
Emanuel 1980 p.475

Lomax, John & Heather
- Charles Kearley house, 'Hat Hill
House', Goodwood, W. Sussex,
1976–7 (now 'Sculpture at
Goodwood')

Lorenz, Erhard
- Ove Arup house, 6 Fitzroy Park,
Highgate N6, 1958 (since extended by
Eva Jiricna)
AD Sept 1958
Harling 1961 pp.102–3

Lovejoy, Derek
- Cariad, Lunghurst Road,
Woldingham 1960
BofE Surrey p.535
- New England (own house),
Lunghurst Road, Woldingham 1960
BofE Surrey p.535
- Addington Hills, Surrey
CL 26 Oct 1972 p.1081

Lucas, Charles
- Warnham Park, Horsham, E. Sussex,
c.1960
Robinson 1984 p.231

Luder, Owen
- Griffith Residence, Wallgrave Rd,
London SW5 (model)
AD Apr 1965 p.184

Lyell, Michael & Associates
- Sir Stanley Unwin house, 4 Oak Hill
Park Estate, London NW3, 1960–2
AR June 1962 pp.430–4
Lambert 1963 p.69
Whiting 1964, pp.11–15

Lyons, Eric
- 2, 4 & 6 Foxes Dale, London SE3, 1957
(No.2 was H&G House of Ideas 1957)
H&G June 1957 pp.36–41
H&G July 1957 pp.25–35

MacKay, Neville
- Coniston Cold Hall, W. Yorkshire,
1972
Robinson 1984 p.205

**Mackenzie, A.G.R.
(A. Marshall Mackenzie & Sons)**
- Candacraig, Aberdeenshire for A.P.F.
Wallace, 1952
Robinson 1984 p.204

Mackie, Ramsay & Taylor
- Loirsbank, Morrison's Bridge,
Aberdeenshire, c.1960
Brogden 1986 p.140

Manasseh, Leonard & Partners
- House at Campden Hill, London W8,
c.1954
H&G Oct 1954 pp.72–3,105
- Bosinney, Fairmile, Surrey, 1958
BofE Surrey p.228
- Own house, 6 Bacon's Lane, London
N6, 1959
ABN 20 Aug 1958
Hope 1963 pp.138–42
Lambert 1963 p.71
Whiting 1964, pp.57–63
Newton 1992 pp.32–37
- 16 South Grove, London N6, 1961
BofE London IV p.408 (overclad)
- Courtyards, Drum House, River Lane,
Petersham, Surrey, 1964–7
BofE Surrey p.411

**Manser, Michael
(with Montague Rayner)**

▸ House at Leatherhead, Surrey, c.1956
Walter 1955/7 pp.82–3

Manser, Michael

▸ 5 Byron Drive, Bishop's Avenue,
London N2, 1962
BofE London 4, p.155

▸ Cliffhanger, Frith Hill, Godalming,
Surrey, c.1963
Whiting 1964 pp.64–67

▸ Own house 'Golden Grove', Forty
Foot Road, Leatherhead, Surrey, 1961
Whiting 1964 pp.68–72

▸ Chaplin house, near Colchester,
Essex, 1963
Jackson p.142

▸ House for Dr Chinery, (Buckland
Cop), Reigate, Surrey, 1966
ABN 10 May 1967 pp.817–20
ABN 20 Sept 1967 pp.522–3
ABN 8 Nov 1967 pp.780–1
AJ 21 May 1969 pp.1371–2

▸ Vickers house, 'Forest Lodge House',
Epsom Road, Epsom, 1966

▸ Pat Fletcher house, Waterlooville,
Hants, 1967
Jackson p.142

▸ Great Lodge House, Ashstead, Surrey,
1967
Jackson p.141

▸ Capel Manor House, Horsmondon,
Kent, 1970
AR Aug 1971 pp.69–72
Bldg 26 May 1972 p.90
Werk July 1972 pp.380–1
H&G Oct 1972 pp.114–7
A&U 1972 No.10 pp.71–76
DBZ June 1973 pp.644–746

**Manser, Michael, & Turnbull,
Peter**

▸ House at Hampstead, London NW3,
1971
H&G March 1972 pp.82–5
IdC No.249 pp.9–14

Sheppard Fidler, A.G.

▸ Herbert Manzoni house,
Birmingham, 1953

Marsh, George

▸ 29 1/2 Loom Lane, Radlett, Herts,
1962–5
Harwood 2000 3.78
Listed Grade II

Marshman, A.A.J.

▸ House at Horton, Northants, 1966
BofE Northamptonshire

Martin, Sir Leslie

▸ Walston house 'Town's End Springs',
Thriplow, Cambs, 1967–70
McKean 1982 p.44
Martin 1983 pp.172–3

Matthew, Stuart

▸ House in Edinburgh
Penn 1954 pp.39, 135

Maufe, Sir Edward

▸ House for Balliol College, Jowett
Walk (cnr College Sports Ground),
Oxford
Smith & Marks (nd) n.p.

Mauger, Paul and Partners

▸ House at Welwyn, Herts, 1955
(Housing Medal Award 1955)
Clifford 1957 p.92

Meacher, Michael

▸ House at Welwyn Garden City, Herts,
1952
Walter 1955/7 p.95

Medd, David & Mary

▸ Own house, 5 Pennyfathers Lane,
Welwyn, Herts, 1954

Meeking, Brian

▸ House adj. railway cutting at
Greenwich, c.1962
Hope 1963 pp.44–7
CL 19 Nov 1964 p.1362

Mein, Henry J.

▸ Stuccoed house at Mansfield, Notts,
1951
Clifford 1957 p.93

Mellor, Tom & Partners

▸ Own house, Lytham St Anne's, Lancs,
1955
Walter 1955/7 pp.16–17

▸ House at Wrea Green, Lancs, c.1956
Clifford 1957 pp.94–5

▸ Own house, Crook, Westmoreland,
1968

**Mellor, Tom & Partners
(Harvey Freeman)**

▸ Howard house 'Riverside', and
adjoining house, Hale, Cheshire,
1966–8
H&G June 1969 pp.68–9
Park, 1971

▸ J. Yates house, Heywood, Gt.
Manchester
ANW Dec 1963–Jan 1964 p.45

Melvin, Peter

▸ Faure house 'Aldbury', Chilterns
ABN 3 April 1968 pp.522–7

Melvin and Lansley

▸ Russell house, Potten End,
Berkhamstead, Herts
ERA Vol.1 No.4 pp.17–21

Melvin and Lansley (P. Mark)

▸ Plant house, 14 New Road, Digswell,
Welwyn Garden City, Herts, 1972
McKean 1982 p.183

Melvin, Lansley & Mark

▸ Eastglade, Rickmansworth, Herts,
1971–4
BofE Herts p.281

Meunier, John

▸ Own house, opp. church, Caldecote,
Cambridgeshire, 1964
AR Aug 1968 p.106
Booth & Taylor 1970 pp.199–200

Meunier, John – see entry under
Gasson, Barry

**Middleton, John (of Dudding,
Middleton and Partners)**

▸ Manor house, Epperstone,
Nottingham
ABN 2 July 1970

**Miller, Keith, and Hucklesby,
Anthony**

▸ Own houses, Toddington, Luton
Bldg 22 Nov 1968 p.83

Mills, Edward D.

▸ House at Walton-on-Thames, Surrey,
1953
Clifford 1957 p.96

▸ Own house and two adjacent houses,
Sydenham, Surrey, 1953
AD April 1954
Clifford 1957 pp.98–9

▸ House at Farnborough Park, Kent,
c.1956
Clifford 1957 p.97

Milne, O.P.

▸ House at Sevenoaks, Kent, 1952
Clifford 1957 p.102

▸ Headmaster's house, Hatch End,
Middlesex, 1953
Clifford 1957 p.101

▸ Lupton Park, Devon, for the 4th Lord
Churston, 1954
CL 26 March 1959
Robinson 1984 p.218

Mock, Rudolf

▸ Mock, Pirie and Littler houses,
Lansdowne Walk, London W11,
c.1954–5
H&G Apr 1955 pp.58–61

▸ Houses at Bawdsey, Suffolk, 1970

Moiret, Peter

▸ Jennings house, Highgate, London
N6
IH November 1965 p.58

Moors

▸ Own house, Kingston upon Thames
H&G Feb 1969 p.53

Morel, Herbert J.

▸ Barrister's house at Bromley, Kent,
1954
Clifford 1957 p.103

▸ House at Scarborough, 1956

Moro, Peter

▸ Own house, 20 Blackheath Park,
Greenwich SE3, 1957–8
AD Sept 1958, pp.347–50
Pidgeon & Crosby 1960 pp.83–8
Lambert 1963 p.93
Emanuel 1980 p.564
Newton 1992 pp.20–25
*CL 31 July 1958; 4 May 2000,
pp.118–121*
Harwood 2000 9.32
Listed Grade II*

▸ Hansen house, Herts, 1968
Emanuel 1980 p.565

**Morris, A.F.C. (Bill) and
Roberts, John**

▸ Brigadier Basil Chichester-Cooke
house, Hammond Place, Upper
Upnor, Rochester, Kent, 1963–4

**Morris and Steedman (James
Morris and Robert Steedman)**

▸ B.C. Tomlinson house, 'Avisfield',
Cramond Road North, Edinburgh,
1956–7, ext 1964

▸ Dentist's house, nr Edinburgh, 1957
Harling 1961 pp.90–1
*Glendinning, Rebuilding Scotland, 1997,
p.118*

▸ Wilson house, 16 Kenock Road,
Lasswade, 1957–8

▸ Robert Steedman and Prof Hunt
houses, Ravelston Dykes Road,
Edinburgh, 1960

▸ Sillitto house, 32 Chaterhall Road,
Edinburgh, 1960

▸ Cheyne house, York Road, North
Berwick, E. Lothian, 1961

▸ Holden House, East Kilbride, S.
Lanarkshire, 1962

▸ Snodgrass house, Mardwell Farm,
Silverburn, Penicuik, Midlothian,
1964

▸ Maurice Berry House, St Thomas
Road, Edinburgh, 1961
Whiting 1964 pp.150–153

**Morris and Steedman
(Robert Steedman)**

▸ Principal's house, University of
Stirling, 1967
Willis 1977 pp.18–21

**Morris and Steedman (James
Shepherd and Eleanor Morris)**

▸ Morris house, Woodcote Park, Fala,
Midlothian, 1970–7
Willis 1977 pp.24–7

Mortimer, Roger

▸ Own house, Bristol
ABN 7 May 1970 pp.30–4

Nelson and Parker

▸ House at Blundellsands, Liverpool
ANW 1966 p.12

▸ Bawden House, Bromborough,
Cheshire
AR Aug 1968 p.105
ANW Apr–May 1969 pp.16–18

▸ Deering house 'Mallards Hey',
Scarisbrick, Lancs, 1964–7
BB Mar 1971 pp.2–9
Bldg 21 May 1971 pp.67–73

Neufeld, Max

▸ 1 Colville Place, London W1, 1964
Listed Grade II

Newberry, Michael & Angela

▸ Own house 'Panshanger', Weare
Street, Capel, Surrey, 1956–7
Pidgeon & Crosby 1960 pp.106–9
Harling 1961 pp.118–19
Jackson 1996, p.137

Newberry, Michael
▸ Own house, Helston, Cornwall 1962
1H *August 1964*
Jackson 1996, p.137

Neylan, Michael
▸ House at Ashstead, Surrey, 1959
Pidgeon & Crosby 1960 pp.96–7

Nicholl, Richard J.
▸ Houses at Welwyn Garden City, 1953

Nops, Colin
▸ Own house, Roundhay, Leeds
YA *1971 no.21 p.475*

Norwood, Douglas & Associates
▸ 25 Cresswell Place, London SW10, 1970
BofE London III p.550

Noscoe, Robin
▸ Own House, Wimborne Minster, Dorset, c.1966

Osman, Louis
▸ Principal's House, Newnham College, Cambridge, 1954–5
1H *Jan 1959 pp.12–16*
CL *4 June 1959 pp.1244–5*
▸ Ranston, Dorset, (reconstruction) for the Gibson-Fleming family, 1961–3
Robinson 1984 pp.188, 223–4
▸ Valley Farm, Edgeworth, Gloucestershire, (reconstruction) for Lady Hollenden, 1970–80
BofE Gloucestershire I, 1999, p.356

Ottewill, David
▸ Own house, 2 Fawn Court, The Ryde, Hatfield, Herts, 1965
Bldg 13 July 1966 pp.65–8
1H *Jun 1967 pp.43–5*

Owers, David
▸ The Paddock, 35 Bar Lane, Stapleford, Cambs, 1974–6

Padovan, Richard
▸ Two flats at 28 Petersham Rd, Richmond, London, 1973
AR *Aug 1972 pp.93–6*
McKean & Jestico 1976 p.82

Pank, Philip – see entry under Howard & Pank

Pank, Philip
▸ Grange Farm, Fingringhoe, Essex
1H *Nov 1970 pp.54–5*

Pank, Goss Associates
▸ 22 Frognal Way, London NW3, 1975–7
BofE London IV p.229

Park, June, & Mardall, Cyril
▸ Own house, Fitzroy Park, London N6, 1949–51 and extension
AR *April 1951*
ADC *Nov 1951*
H&G *Oct 1954 pp.70–1, 105*
Penn 1954 pp.32–3
1H *Dec 1967 p.42*

Park, June
▸ House at Moor Park, Herts, 1954
Clifford 1957 pp.104–5

Parker, J. Roy (see also under Nelson & Parker)
▸ Own house, 1 Ingestre Road, Oxton, Merseyside, 1956 (with later extensions)
▸ House at Boundary Road (corner Upton Road), Bidston, Cheshire, 1957
AD *Oct 1957 p.376*
▸ Charleville, Eleanor Road, Birkenhead, Cheshire, 1959
▸ C.V. Brown house, Bidston, Birkenhead, Cheshire
ANW *Dec 1963–Jan 1964 p.44*

Parr, James
▸ The Rock, Dundee Road, West Ferry, Dundee, 1963
McKean & Walker 1984 p.105
▸ Own house, 95 Dundee Road, West Ferry, Dundee, 1964
McKean & Walker 1984 p.105

Pattrick, Michael
▸ House on Beaulieu River, Hants, c.1962
▸ Richard and Phoebe Merricks beach house, Pett Level, Kent, c.1968
Harling 1961 pp.28–31

Peake, Brian (Michael E. Woodford)
▸ Own house, Otham, nr Maidstone, Kent, c.1953
H&G *Feb 1954 pp.46–9, 94*

Peake, Brian
▸ House in Hampstead, London NW3, c.1962
Hope 1963 pp.148–50
▸ Black house, Tunbridge Wells, Kent, c.1960
Hope 1963 pp.151–3
ABN *14 Apr 1965 pp.705–6*

Pearlman, Wolf
▸ 6 Ringley Drive, Whitefields, Manchester, 1968–9

Penn, Colin
▸ House at Gerrard's Cross, Bucks
Penn 1954 pp.37, 51

Penn, John
▸ House at Hasketon, Suffolk, 1961
▸ Audrey Penn house, Bawdsey Hall, Suffolk, 1962–3
▸ Mrs Hanson house, 'Garden House', Broomheath, Woodbridge, Suffolk, 1963–4
▸ Wing Commander Everson house, 'Takoradi', Ufford, Suffolk, 1964–5
▸ John A. Barnham house, 'Churchmeadow', Rendham, Suffolk, 1965–6
▸ Mr & Mrs Robert Taylor house, 'Sartoria', Bruisyard Road, Rendham, Suffolk, 1966–7
▸ Colin Graham house, 'Lion House', Ferry Road, Orford, Suffolk, 1967–8
▸ LaForge house, 'Beach House', Shingle Street, Suffolk, 1967–72
▸ Mrs Richard Longe house, 'Hasketon Lodge', Hasketon, Woodbridge, Suffolk, 1967–8
▸ Mr & Mrs Peter Youngman house, 'Fenstreet', Fenstreet Road, Westleton, Suffolk, 1969–71

Penoyre, John & Jane
▸ House at Rosemont Road, Richmond, Surrey, 1963
Whiting 1964 pp.109–13

Phillimore, Claude
▸ Belsay House (alias Swanstead), Northumberland, for Sir Stephen Middleton Bt, 1946–7
Robinson 1984 p.201
BofE Northumberland, 1992, pp.169–70
▸ Llysdinam, Radnorshire (reconstruction), for Sir Michael Dillwyn-Venables-Llewelyn, Bt, 1954
BoW Powys p.357
Robinson 1984 pp.216–7
▸ Arundel Park, Arundel, for 16th Duke of Norfolk, W. Sussex, 1958–62
Connoisseur June 1963 pp.72–83
Robinson 1984
▸ Abercairney, Crieff, Perthshire, for Major J. Drummond-Moray, c.1960
Robinson 1984 p.197
▸ Tusmore Park, Oxfordshire, for 2nd Lord Bicester, 1961–2 (demolished)
Robinson 1984 p.230
▸ Ribblesdale Park, Ascot, Berkshire, for J.R. Hindley, 1961–4
Robinson 1984 p.224
▸ Bartlow Park, Cambridgeshire, for Brig A.N. Breitmeyer, 1962
▸ Knowsley, Lancashire, for 17th Earl of Derby, 1963
Robinson 1984 pp.126, 215
▸ High Beeches, Handcross, E. Sussex, for the Hon Edward Boscawen, 1966
Robinson 1984 p.213
▸ Cubberley, Herefordshire, for 4th Lord Greville, 1966–7
Robinson 1984 p.206
▸ Basing House, Privett, Hampshire, for James Langmead, 1968–70
Robinson 1984 p.201
▸ Horsted Keynes, E. Sussex, for Julian Faber, 1971
Robinson 1984 p.213

Phillips, Derek
▸ W.E. Bailey house, Hemel Hempstead
Bldg 31 May 1968 pp.63–5

Phillips, Michael, and Cutler, Derek
▸ Own houses, Wolverhampton
Bldg 7 July 1972 pp.55–9

Pilley, A.V.
▸ Varsanyi house, London NW3, c.1952
H&G *Aug 1953 pp.32–3, 67*

Pinckney, Roger & Gott, Arthur
▸ Sevenhampton Place, Wiltshire, for Ian Fleming, 1963
Robinson 1984 pp.225–6

Planning Design Group
▸ John Shelley house by the Thames at Cookham, Middlesex

Pollen, Francis – see also entry under Brett & Pollen

Pollen, Francis
▸ Own house 'The Walled Garden', Henley-on-Thames, Oxon, 1958
CL *10 Nov 1960 pp.1121–2*
Powers 1999 p.67
▸ Arthur Pollen house 'Cray Clearing', Harpsden Wood, Henley-on-Thames, Oxon, 1962–4 (demolished 1995)
CL *6 April 1967 pp.768–9*
BofE 'Oxfordshire' pp.406, 635
Powers 1999 pp.67–73
▸ House at North End, nr Christmas Common, Watlington, Oxon, 1965
Powers 1999 p.77
▸ John Baring house 'Lake House', The Grange, Northington, Hants, 1971–5
Powers 1999 pp.73–6
▸ Fletcher house, 'Field House', Combe, Berks, 1972
Powers 1999 p.78
▸ Goldstein house, 'Pool House', Sonning, Berks, 1975
Powers 1999 p.79

Potter, Alexander
▸ Gorsfach, Pennant, Dyfed, 1975

Potter, F.
▸ Avon Lock, Tewkesbury, Gloucs.
Bldg 17 May 1968 pp.87–8

Pottinger, T.O.
▸ Jay house, Manley, Cheshire
1H *Nov 1968 pp.34–5*

Powell, Sir Philip, & Moya, Hidalgo
▸ Two houses in Mount Lane, West Gate, Chichester, W. Sussex, 1949–50
AD *April 1951*
Mills 1953 pp.55–62
▸ Howell Leadbeater and Desmond Keeling houses 'Milk Wood' & 'Headlong Hill', Stokes Heath Road, Oxshott, Surrey, 1951–4
H&G *Nov 1957 pp.85–7*
Walter 1955/7 pp.54–5
▸ Monica and Muriel Anthony house, Toys Hill, nr Westerham, Kent, 1954
H&G *May 1955 pp.72–5*
Walter 1955/7 pp.36–9
▸ House (for Mrs Moya) at Leamington Spa, Warwickshire, 1956 (demolished)
Emanuel 1980 p.641

Prangnell, Peter
▸ Own house, nr Medway, North Downs, Kent, c.1956–7
H&G *Jan 1957 pp.32–5*

Ratcliffe, C.B.

▸ House at Grovewood Close, Chorley Wood, Bucks, 1954
Walter 1955/7 pp.43–5

Rayson, Thomas

▸ Dower house, Letcombe Regis, Berkshire, for Major Carlton-Crosse, 1958
Clifford 1963 pp.104–6
Robinson 1984 p.216

Readman, Stuart C.

▸ House at Hockley, Essex, 1956
Walter 1955/7 p.76

Redfern, Alan

▸ Ladycroft Paddock, Allestree, Derbyshire, c.1969

Reid, John & Sylvia

▸ House, Borrow Road, Oulton Broad, Suffolk, 1954

▸ Wiegerinck house, Lowestoft, Suffolk, 1953–5
H&G March 1956 pp.66–9
Walter 1955/7 pp.70–1
Clifford 1957 pp.106–7

**Reid, Paul
(of Leslie Martin office)**

▸ House in village street, Great Shelford, Cambs, 1963–4

Rendle, Timothy

▸ 14 Willow Avenue, London SW13, 1967–8
BofE London 2, pp.467–8
AR Dec 1969 pp.467–8

▸ House at 23 Strand on the Green, London W4, 1966
AR Sept 1967 pp.219–21
McKean & Jestico 1976 p.79

Renton, Stuart

▸ Own house, Nether Liberton, Edinburgh, c.1960
Harling 1961 pp.6, 72–3

Reynish, R. Lewis

▸ House at Bedhampton, Hants
Br 6 Jan 1956 pp.923, 933

**Richardson & Houfe,
(Prof. Albert E. Richardson &
E.A.S. Houfe)**

▸ James White house, Bromham Road, Bedford, 1953–4
CL 20 Oct 1955 pp.856–7
Clifford 1957 pp.108–10

▸ Principal's Lodging, St Hilda's College, Oxford, 1954
AJ, CXXXVI 1957, p.58
Br CIC 1961 p.61; CC 1961 p.593

**Richardson, Houfe & Partners
(design by Houfe)**

▸ Capt Oscar Dixon house, Kenwick Hall, Legbourne, Lincolnshire,1960
Robinson 1984 pp.65, 214
BofE Lincolnshire 1989 p.433

Richardson, Houfe & Partners

▸ Weston Patrick house, Hants, 1956–8
CL 13 Oct 1960 pp.816–8

**Richardson, Houfe & Partners
(design by Houfe)**

▸ Vicarage at Cardington, Beds, c.1966

**Richmond, Martin
(with Arthur Baker)**

▸ Doctor's house and Surgery, Hampton, 1958
Harling 1961 pp.96–7

▸ Three terrace houses at Kensington, London SW7, c.1962
Hope 1963 pp.143–4

Rix, N. & M.E.

▸ Own house, Bromley, Kent, 1954
Clifford 1957 pp.111

Roberts, David

▸ Own house, 11 Wilberforce Road, Cambridge, 1952–7
McKean 1982 p.18

Roberts, Keith

▸ Own house, Camden Square, London NW1
IH Mar 1968 pp.90–1

Roberts, Francis

▸ 3 The Triangle, Preston, Lancs, 1962; 1976–8; 1989–93

Robotham, D.H.

▸ House at Snitterfield, Warwicks, 1966–73
D. Hickman Shell Guide

**Robotham, Matthew &
Associates**

▸ Standen Farmhouse, Yarwell Road, Wansford, Cambs, 1973
McKean 1982 p.64

Rock, David

▸ Extension to a Span house, Putney, London
Bldg 26.7.1968 pp.87–9

Rogers, Richard and Su

▸ House for Dr Rogers, 22 Parkside, Wimbledon, London SW19, 1970
AJ 6 Oct 1971 pp.753–66
B&W 1970 no.12 pp.442–3
PA May 1972 pp.116–9
IH June 1972 pp.48–51
A&U 1972 no.10 pp.65–70
McKean & Jestico 1976 p.64
Powell 1999 pp.72–81

▸ Humphrey Spender house 'The Studio', Ulting, Maldon, Essex, 1966–8
AJ 6 Oct 1971 pp.753–66
CL 23 Sept 1969 pp.114–9
Powell 1999 pp.68–71

Rose, Malcolm

▸ Own house, Norwich
ERA May–June 1971 pp.14–5

Rothermel, Rolf

▸ Own house, Little Baddow, Essex
A Feb 1971 pp.40–2
ID Jan 1971 pp.18–19

Rottenberg, Gerson

▸ 29 Flask Walk and Lakis Close, London NW3, 1973
BofE London IV, p.223

Russell, Barry

▸ Own house, 'Crossroads House', Charlton, W. Sussex, 1969

Ryder, Gordon (with Jack Lynn)

▸ Dr W. Walker house, 20 Wolsingham Park South, Newcastle upon Tyne, 1952

Ryder & Yates

▸ Derek Damerell house 'Harlequin', Gill Road, Scotby, Carlisle, Cumbria, 1954
AR Nov 1956
H&G May 1957 pp.64–7

▸ Hill House Farm, Walton, Brampton, Cumbria, 1954

▸ 52 and 68 Brierdene Crescent, Whitley Bay, 1956

▸ J.F. Tonner house 'Friars Garth', Hayton, Carlisle, Cumbria, 1956 (Civic Trust award winner)

▸ Charles Oakley house additions, South View, Hayton Townhead, Cumbria, 1957

▸ D.M.C. Saint house and surgery, Longbenton, Newcastle upon Tyne, 1957

▸ John Liddel house, 1F Grand Parade, Tynemouth, North Tyneside, Tyne & Wear, 1958
AR Aug 1956 pp.105–7

▸ Alice Marmourian house, Stanton Hide, Stanton, Northumberland, 1959
Br 22 July 1960 pp.138–9
NA Sept 1964 p.396

Ryder, J. Gordon

▸ Own house 'Trees', Middle Drive, Wolsington, Newcastle upon Tyne, 1967–8
AR Jan 1968 p.83
H&G Feb 1972 pp.46–50
ID May 1973 pp.324–5

St Leger, Julian

▸ St Leger house, Harlow
ABN 27 Apr 1966 pp.257–8

Samuel, Edward & Stella

▸ Own house on site of and using material from former Hornsey Town Hall, London N6, c.1952–7
H&G Dec 1957 pp.75–7
Harling 1961 pp.115–17

▸ Casdagli house, Wigginton, Tring, Herts, c.1962
Harling 1963 pp.96–7

▸ 1 Aylmer Close, Stanmore, Harrow, 1963
Harwood 2000 7.68
Listed Grade II

Samuel, Edward & Partners

▸ House, Shalford, Essex, 1967
AR 1967 pp.222–4
ABN 24 Apr 1968 pp.638–9

Sandys, Jennifer

▸ Own house, 'The High House', Winchester Road, Stroud, Hants, 1964

**Saunders, Frank & Partners
(C. Huggins)**

▸ House at Upper Somerton, Suffolk, 1972
McKean 1982 p.103

Scott, W. Schomberg

▸ Membland, Haddington, E. Lothian, for Admiral Sir Peter Reid, 1966
Robinson 1984 p.219

▸ Rawfleet, Roxburghshire, 1960s
Robinson 1984 p.223

▸ Crathes, Kincardinshire, for Mr Burnett of Leys, 1970 (completion)
Robinson 1984 p.206

▸ Dupplin Castle, Forteviot, for 2nd Lord Forteviot, 1970
Robinson 1984 pp.117, 208

▸ Gannochy Lodge, Edzell, Angus, 1973
Robinson 1984 pp.119, 209

Schwerdt, John

▸ House in Park Road, Lewes, E. Sussex, c.1960

▸ House at Firle, E. Sussex, c.1960

▸ Sidney Horniblow house, 'White Fox Lodge', Udimore, Rye, E. Sussex, 1964–5
Harwood 2000 6.32
Listed Grade II

Scorer, Sam

▸ Wright house (converted air raid shelter)
IH 1971 Sept pp.86–7

▸ Own house, 7 Gibralter Hill, Lincoln, c.1975

Scott, Sir Giles Gilbert

▸ 'Boxgrove' house (standard design), George Road, Coombe Hill, Kingston upon Thames, Surrey, c.1950

Scott, Brownrigg and Turner

▸ House at Guildford, Surrey
TB 3 Jan 1964 p.19

Seal, Mervyn

▸ House at Torquay, Devon
IH June 1967 pp.40–2

Segal, Walter

▸ Schultz house, Lawrence Road, The Ridgeway, Mill Hill, Barnet, 1947

▸ Houses at 1–8 St Anne's Close, London N6, 1951–2

▸ House, Crooked Usage, Finchley, London, 1951–61
Emanuel 1980 p.733

▸ Weil house, 16 & 18 Neeld Crescent, London NW4, 1950s
Emanuel 1980 p.733

▸ House, Dennis Avenue, Stanmore, Middlesex, 1950s
Emanuel 1980 p.733

▸ 2 & 4 Woodville Road, Brent, London, 1953
Emanuel 1980 p.733

▸ B. Rowley house, 15 The Boltons, London SW10, 1957 (demolished)
Emanuel 1980 p.733

▸ House, Church Road, Bushill Park, London N19, 1950s
Emanuel 1980 p.733

▸ A.H. Rowley house, 432 Church Street, Enfield, 1958

▸ Gult house, 79 West Heath Gardens, London NW3, 1961
AD Nov 1953 pp.315–16

▸ Tobler house, Rugby Road, Twickenham, Richmond, 1959–61
Emanuel 1980 p.733

▸ Own 'Temporary' house, 9 North Hill, London N6, 1963–5
AJ 23 March 1966 p.763
AJ 4 May 1988 pp.64–9
Newton 1992 pp.50–7

▸ 4, 5 & 5A Tasker Road, London NW5, 1963

▸ Own house, 9 North Hill, London N6, 1967
ABN 23 Oct 1968
Newton pp.50–7

▸ Collier house, 'Tree House', 30 Chapel Street, Halstead, Essex, 1969
AJ 20 Sept 1970 p.769
Emanuel 1980 p.733

▸ Leigh house, Main Street, Yelling, Cambs, 1969–70
AJ 20 Sept 1970 p.769
Emanuel 1980 p.733

▸ Additions to 'Phantom Ranch', North Chailey, Lewes, E. Sussex, 1969–70
AJ 20 Sept 1970 p.769
Emanuel 1980 p.733

▸ Cook house, Warrenorth, N. Common, nr Chailey, Lewes, E. Sussex, 1971

▸ Godfrey house & studio, Chapel Lane, Clifford, Boston Spa, W. Yorks, 1972

▸ Birch house, 'Telfs', Hendon Wood Lane, Barnet NW7, 1975

▸ Green house, Kennell Hill, Sharnbrook, Beds, 1979

Sharp, Derek

▸ House at The Avenue, Beckenham, Kent
AD Jan 1968 p.17 (project)

▸ Manor House, Frimley, Surrey
AD Jan 1968 p.17 (project)

▸ House at Snakes Lane, Woodford Green, Essex
AD Jan 1968 p.17 (project)

▸ House at 3 Farm End, Chingford, Waltham Forest, London E4
AD Jan 1968 p.17 (project)

▸ Davis House, Churt, Surrey
AD Jan 1968 p.17 (project)

▸ House at 8 Baldwins Lane, Loughton, Essex
AD Jan 1968 p.17 (project)

Shaw-Stewart, Blaikie & Perry (Frank Perry)

▸ A.L. Norman house, Newlands Farm, Near Gifford, East Lothian, 1960–61
Whiting 1964 pp.123–9

Shelley, David

▸ Stainsby House, Derbyshire, 1972–4
Robinson 1984 p.227–8

Shepheard, Sir Peter (Shepheard, Epstein & Hunter)

▸ Own house, 21 Well Road, London NW3, c.1975

Sheppard, Richard and Partners (Gordon Taylor)

▸ Cyril Sweett house 'High Pine', Storrington, W. Sussex, 1954
Walter 1955/7 pp.56–8

Shirbon, W.A.

▸ House at Scarborough, Yorkshire, 1953
Clifford 1957 pp.112–3

▸ Own house, Stoke d'Abernon, Surrey
Clifford 1957 p.114

Shorten, Derek

▸ Own house, 71 Whitney Drive, Stevenage, Herts 1966

Siddons, W.R.

▸ 37 Cresswell Place, London SW10, c.1970
BofE London III p.550

Simmons, R.G.

▸ House at Esher, Surrey, 1953–4
Clifford 1957 pp.116–7

Sims, Ronald G.

▸ House at Acomb, York
YA Mar–Apr 1969 pp.108–9

▸ Dalby Hall, Terrington, York
YA Mar–Apr 1969 pp.106–7

▸ House at Strensall, York
YA Mar–Apr 1969 pp.104–5

Sisson, Marshall

▸ Okeover Hall, Staffordshire, for Sir Ian Walker-Okeover, Bt, 1957–60
CL 23 Jan & 12 Mar 1964
Robinson 1984 pp.68, 221

Smith, Cecil

▸ Hockering Hall, Norfolk, for John Verel, 1968
Robinson 1984 p.213

Smith, K.R. (of Atkinson, Smith & Haywood)

▸ 'South Deep' (Catchpole house) and 'Wingate' (own house), Stratford Road, Watford, Herts, 1956–8

Smith, F. Beresford

▸ Own house, Bath
Br 25 January 1957 p.177

Smith, Graham, & Robinson, E.H.

▸ Peter Linton house, 'Hysol', Tye Green, Harlow, Essex, c.1960, ext 1963

Smith, Raymond

▸ Infill house at Greenwich, c.1960
Harling 1961 p.114
Hope 1963 pp.67–71

Smithson, Alison & Peter

▸ Derek Sugden house, 2 Farm Field, Devereux Drive, Watford, Herts, 1954–7
AR Sep.1957, pp.194–7
AD June 1958 p.240
H&G Dec 1957 p.45
A&P Smithson 'The Shift' 1982 pp.86–7
BofE 1977 p.460
AJ 26 June 1997

▸ Wayland Young Garden pavilion, 100 Bayswater Road, London W2, 1959
AR May 1960
Whiting 1964 pp.104–108

▸ Caro house, Frognal, London NW3
Emanuel 1980 p.759

▸ Own house 'Fonthill Folly', Upper Lawn, Tisbury, 1962 (additions)
AR Feb 1963 pp.135–6

Sofaer, Julian

▸ Whiles house, Sandford Drive, near Wareham, Dorset, 1954–55
Whiting 1964 pp.135–137

▸ House at Blackheath Hill, London SE10
AR Aug 1968 pp.110–11

Sørensen, Eric

▸ Dr Kennard house 'Keelson', 8a Hills Avenue, Cambridge, 1960–1
AR May 1962 pp.311–14
H&G July 1963 pp.68–71
Booth & Taylor 1970 pp.86–7
McKean 1982 p.41
Murray & Trombley 1990 pp.12–13
Harwood 2000 3.64
Listed Grade II

Spence, Sir Basil & Partners

▸ House at Longniddry, East Lothian, c.1953–5
Penn 1954 pp.56, 107
Edwards 1995 p.102

▸ Schoolkeeper's house for the L.C.C., Sydenham School, Dartmouth Road, Lewisham SE23, 1954
Clifford 1957 p.118

▸ Wray house, Wimbledon, London SW19, 1958
Emanuel 1980 p.767
Edwards 1995 p.102

▸ Own house Tarks Reach, Dock Lane, Beaulieu, Hants, 1961
AR March 1962 pp.168–74
BofE Hants & IoW 1973 p.97
Edwards 1995 pp.81, 102
Harwood 2000 5.28
Listed Grade II

Spence, Robin (Spence & Webster)

▸ D.C. Pine house, Main Street, Thornton, Leicestershire
AJ 24 May 1972 pp.1139–54

Spence, Robin

▸ Murray house at Hamilton Rd West, Old Hunstanton, Norfolk, 1971
AJ 24 May 1972 pp.1139–54
Jackson 1996 p.152

Spencer and Gore

▸ 'White Lodge', Linton, near Maidstone, Kent, 1959
Pidgeon & Crosby 1960 pp.102–3
Harling 1961 pp.76–7

Stammers, J.R.

▸ Juneberry, Alders Road, Reigate, Surrey, 1955
BofE Surrey p.431

Stansfield Smith, Colin

▸ House at Petersham, Kingston upon Thames, Surrey
AJ 26 Aug 1970 p478

Stead, Peter

▸ House at 4 Arkenley Lane, Alconbury Common, Huddersfield, W. Yorks, 1957–63
Bruckman & Lewis 1960 pp.116–7
Synthesis 1994

Stead, Peter & Lewis, David (of Design Collaborative)

▸ 'Fairways', 8 Almondbury Common, Almondbury, Huddersfield, W. Yorks, 1959
AD Sep.1964 pp.449–51
Pidgeon & Crosby 1960 pp.110–13
Synthesis 1994

Stead, Peter

▸ Own house, 'Berry Brow', Carriage Drive, Armitage Bridge, Huddersfield, W. Yorks, 1968
Synthesis 1994

Stean, Shipman & Cantacuzino (Sherban Cantacuzino)

▸ Max Bygraves house, Pachesham Park, Pentice Walk, Leatherhead, Surrey, 1960–2
CL 19 Sep.1963 pp.696–7
H&G Dec–Jan 1973–74 pp.80–3

Steedman, Robert – see entry under Morris and Steedman

Stephen, Douglas

▸ House at East Horsley, Surrey, 1954
Emanuel 1980 p.771

▸ Neoclassical house [sic], London NW3, 1973
Emanuel 1980 p.771

Stephenson, Arthur

▸ House at Weybridge, Surrey, 1959
Harling 1961 pp.48–9

Stern, David

▸ 88 West Heath Road, NW3, 1966
BofE London IV p.139

▸ 6 Golder's Park Close, NW11, 1966
BofE London IV p.138

Stevens, Donald (of Stevens, Giddens & Partners)

▸ Richard Thirlby house, on River Medina, West Cowes, IoW, c.1966
Harling 1961 pp.52–3

Stillman, C.G. (Middlesex County Architect)

▸ Own house, 8 Fitzroy Park, Highgate N6
AJ 7 May 1953

Stillman & Eastwick-Field

▸ House near Midhurst, W. Sussex
Penn 1954 pp.31, 39

Stillman & Eastwick-Field

▸ House at Reigate, Surrey
Penn 1954 pp.59, 89

Stirling & Gowan (James Gowan)

▸ House at Baring Road, Cowes, IoW, 1955–7
AR April 1958
AJ 24 July, 31 July 28 Aug & 4 Sept 1958
AD Sept 1958
H&G Nov 1958
Pidgeon & Crosby 1960 pp.80–2
Harling 1961 pp.94–5
Rowe (ed) 1984 pp.55–6, 334

▸ House at Grenville Place, London SW7, 1957–59
Daily Telegraph 19 Jan 1960
AR Mar 1960
ABN 20 July 1960
Hope 1963 pp.52–4
Rowe (ed) 1984 pp.57–8, 334

Stone, G.

▸ Hall house, Leamington Spa, Warwks
IH Nov 1965 p.58

Stout & Litchfield

▸ Milton Grundy house, Shipton-under-Wychwood, Oxon, 1964
AR Feb 1965 pp.144–6
DBZ Nov 1965 pp.967ff.
CL 3 Nov 1966 p.1135
Bouw 14 Jan 1967 pp.70–2
BM May 1967 pp.592
BofE Oxon pp.406, 760
Harling 1968 pp.12–15
Murray & Trombley 1990 p.138–9
Harwood 2000 5.44
Listed grade II

▸ Gillian Jacomb-Hood house, South Harting, E. Sussex, c.1968
ABN 11 Jan 1967 pp.65–6
[H]&G June 1967 pp.44–6
[   ] 1971 no.7 pp.35–8
[   ]kt Vol.8 June 1971
[   ]68 pp.16–19

▸ [   ]gsdown Street, London
[   ]–9
[   ]–7
[   ]

▸ House at Pimlico, London SW1
AR 1972 pp.162–5
H&G May 1972 pp.90–3
BD Nov 1972 p.18

▸ House at Highgate, London N6
AR Aug 1971 pp.84–6

▸ Nolan house, Worcester Park, Surrey
AR Aug 1968 p.108
A&U 1970 pp.31–3
IdC No.249 pp.3–7

▸ 20A Bishopswood Road, London N6, c.1973
BofE London IV p.412

▸ 'Kingfishers', The Drive, Kingston upon Thames, 1977
BofE London II p.320

Stutchbury, Wycliffe

▸ House for mother, 'Gayles Orchard', Eastdean, Sussex
CL Feb 15 1968 p.334–5

Summers, Royston

▸ House at Esher, Surrey
H&G Oct 1971 pp.118–21

Sykes, Elsworth

▸ House at Ferriby, E.Yorks
Perspective Nov–Dec 1964 p.136

Sylvester, Martin

▸ House for Martin Gilbert, Oxford
H&G Nov 1969 pp.72–7

▸ House for Dr Werner Fladée, nr Maidenhead, Berks
H&G Sept 1971 pp.80–3

Tarren and Caller

▸ House at Woolsington, Newcastle upon Tyne
NA Sept 1964 p.397

Tayler & Green

▸ Imhof House,'Robin Hill', Coombe Hill Road, Kingston upon Thames, 1943–8, extended 1966
Mills 1953 pp.17–25
Penn 1954 pp.142–3
Powers 1998 pp.25–6

▸ F. Jenkins house 'North Landing', Borrow Road, Oulton Broad, Suffolk, 1949–51
ABN 31 May 1956 p.598
AJ 31 May 1956 p.613
H&G Sept 1957 p.69
CL 9 Oct 1958 pp.790–2
Stuttgart, 1956, p.139
Mauger 1959 p.206
Harling 1961 p.54
Gresswell 1964 p.21
Harwood & Powers 1998 pp.75, 91; also n.p

▸ Stuart Craik house, 94 Corton Road, Lowestoft, Norfolk, 1955
Gresswell 1964 p.50
Harwood & Powers 1998 p.96

▸ Frederick Lynch house, Tunney's Lane, Ditchingham, Norfolk, 1961–3

Taylor, John (of Chapman Taylor & Partners)

▸ Castle Gyrn, Clwyd, Wales, 1977
Robinson 1984 pp.21, 204

Taylor, J.R.B.

▸ Taylor House, 3 South Lane, Comberton, Cambridge, 1965–6
Booth & Taylor 1970 pp.198–9

Taylor and Crowther

▸ House at Truro, Cornwall, 1953
Walter 1955/7 p.91

▸ House nr Feock, Cornwall, 1955–6
Walter 1955/7 p.61
Clifford 1957 p.119

▸ House at Truro, Cornwall, 1956
Walter 1955/7 pp.66–7

Taylor and Hunt

▸ J.L. Schulz house, Newland Park, Hull, E. Yorks
Perspective Nov–Dec 1964 p.135

Taylor, Maurice

▸ Own house, Highbury Terrace, Highbury, London N5
AJ 26 Aug 1970 pp.470–2
IH Sept 1971 pp.52–5

Team 4 (Norman & Wendy Foster and Richard & Su Rogers)

▸ Marcus & Rene Brumwell house 'Creek Vean', Feock, Truro, Cornwall, 1964–6
AR Aug 1968 pp.95–6
Appleyard 1986
Foster 1991 I pp.36–45
Powell 1999 pp.28–37
Harwood 2000 4.24
Listed Grade II

▸ Houses at 15, 17 and 19 Murray Mews, London NW1, 1964–5
Appleyard 1986
Foster 1991 I pp.52–7
Jones & Woodward 1992 p.61
Powell 1999 pp.44–49

▸ Jaffe house 'Skybreak House', The Warren, Radlett, Herts 1965–6 (Interior used in Kubrick's 'A Clockwork Orange')
Werk (Zurich) 1969 no.1 pp.38–41
AR Aug 1968 p.97
Einzig 1981
McKean 1982 p.171
Foster 1991 I pp.66–71
Powell 1999 pp.40–43

Thomas, Bryan

▸ House at Fordham Heath, Essex
H&G Vol.28 Apr 1973 pp.120–3

Thomas, Dewi Prys

▸ Professor J. Banks house 'Entwood', 18 Westwood Road, Noctorum, Birkenhead, Cheshire, 1959
BofE Cheshire 1971 p105
Harwood 2000 1.44
Listed Grade II

Thomas Morgan Associates

▸ 30 Windsor Road, Radyr, Cardiff, 1968

Thompson, B.E.

▸ Sheffield (Swedish 'Boro' system timber framed housing)
Wood Aug–Sept 1969 pp.12–15
ABN 1 Jan 1970 pp.50–3

Tischler, F.

▸ 38 Between Street, Cobham, Surrey, 1954
BofE Surrey p.164

Townsend, John

▸ 43 Murray Mews, London NW1, 1974–5
BofE London IV p.391

Townsend, Robert

▸ House at Durrington, Wilts
AJ 26 March 1953 pp.401–3

▸ House at Gt Somerford, Wilts 1953

▸ Doctor's house 'Robinswood', Broughton Road, Banbury, Oxon, designed 1939, built 1952–3 (demolished)
Penn 1954 p.62, 72

▸ House at Gastard, Corsham, Wilts, 1953–4
Walter 1955/7 pp.100–1

▸ 23 Hintlesham Avenue, Harborne, Birmingham, 1955

Trebilcock, Ronald

▸ Lucie Manen house 'Five Limes', 48a Netherhall Gardens, London NW3, c.1962
Hope 1963 pp.38–43

Turner, Kenneth

▸ Three houses at Upper Batley, W. Yorks, 1960
Schmitt pp.124–7

Tye, Geoffrey

▸ Own house, Great West Plantation, Tring, Herts, 1975
Herts 1979 p.48

Uffindell and Holgate

▸ Own houses, St Mary Platt, Kent, 1953–4
Clifford 1957 p.120

Upton, A.

▸ House at Putney Hill, London SW15, 1956
Walter 1955/7 p.94

Utzon, Jørn (sketch design)

▸ Povl Ahm House, 44 West Common Way, Harpenden, Herts, 1961–3; and addition by Ulrick Plesner in association with Christopher Beaver Associates 1972–4
CL 17 March 1966 pp.608–10
BofE Herts 1977 p.158
Harwood 2000 3.74
Listed Grade II

Van Heyningen & Haward

▸ 24 York Rise, London NW5, 1975
BofE London IV p.402

Ventris, Michael & Lois

▸ Own house, 19 North End, London NW3, 1953
CL 12 Nov 1959
H&G Feb 1955 pp.48–51
Park 1958 pp.42–3

Voelcker, John

▸ Humphrey Lyttelton house, Alyn Close, Barnet Road, Arkley, Herts, 1958–9
  H&G 1958 p.51
  AJ 23 Jan 1958
  AR May 1960 pp.319–21

Walker, Derek

▸ Rodney Kent house, 'Villa Capri', Fulwith Road, Harrogate, W. Yorks, 1959

▸ Johnson House, North Rigton, N. Yorks, 1964
  Emanuel 1980 p.861

Walker, Derek (with Duncan Biggin)

▸ Churnin House, Collingham, W. Yorks, c.1962
  Harling 1963 pp.100–1
  Emanuel 1980 p.861

▸ Gould House, Leeds, W. Yorks, 1966
  Emanuel 1980 p.861

▸ David Serenson house 'Calder Point', Calderstones, Liverpool
  Glass Age May 1973 pp.28–9
  AD Jan 1967 pp.14–15

Walker, Derek, Attenborough, John, & Jones, Bryn

▸ Gould House, Leeds, W. Yorks
  AD Apr 1966 pp.183–4
  AD Jan 1969 pp.53–4

Walter, Felix

▸ House at Walberswick for wheelchair-bound client, Suffolk, 1950
  Penn 1954 p.130
  Walter 1955/7 pp.96–8

Wallis, M.

▸ Own House, Bengeo, Herts, 1953
  Walter 1955/7 pp.88–9

Ward, Basil (of Murray, Ward & Partners)

▸ Matson Ground, Windermere, Cumbria, for Peter Scott, 1961
  BofE Cumberland & Westmoreland p.230
  Robinson 1984 p.219

Warwick, Ian

▸ House at Risinghoe Castle, Renhold, nr Castle Mill Farm, Beds, 1954
  Walter 1955/7 pp.26–7

Wearden, Clifford

▸ Noonamena House, Onslow Road, Burwood Park, Weybridge, Surrey, 1953
  Emanuel 1980 p.871

▸ Service house, Inchmery, Exbury Estate, Hants, 1958
  Emanuel 1980 p.861

Weeks, John

▸ House at Mayfield, Surrey, 1955
  Emanuel 1980 p.872

Weeks, John and Huckstepp, Michael

▸ House nr Woking, Surrey, 1956
  Harling, 1961, pp.68–9

Wiess, John

▸ Wiess house, Parliament Hill, London NW3, 1961 (extended by Maurice Myerson 1971)
  Newton 1992 pp.38–43

Westwood, Piet and Partners (Brian & Norman Westwood)

▸ Riverside bungalow for John Schilling, Weybridge, Surrey
  ABN 6 Apr 1966 pp.605–6
  Bldg 20 Jan 1967 pp.74–6

Widdup, F. Macfarlane – see entry under Dunham, Widdup & Harrison

Williams, J.C.

▸ House at Hythe, Hampshire, 1957

Williams-Ellis, Sir Clough (with Lionel Brett)

▸ Doctor's house, Weston-super-Mare, Somerset
  Emanuel 1980 p.889

Williams-Ellis, Sir Clough

▸ Lloyd-Price house, Rhiwlas, Merioneth, Gwynedd, 1954
  Robinson 1984 pp.95, 224

▸ Wynne-Finch house, Voelas, Denbighshire, Clwyd, 1958
  Robinson 1984 pp.94, 230

▸ Sir Vivyan Naylor-Leyland house, Nantclwyd Hall, Denbighshire, Clwyd, 1957–74 (reconstruction)
  Robinson 1984 p.96

▸ House near Llanfaelrhys, Caernarvonshire
  Emanuel 1980 p.889

▸ Home Farm House, Aston Tyrrold Manor, Berks
  Emanuel 1980 p.889

▸ Crown house and gardens, Barford St John, Oxon
  Emanuel 1980 p.889

▸ Anthony Mason-Hornby house, Dalton Hall, Westmoreland, 1968–71
  Robinson 1984 p.98

Williamson, Faulkner Brown and Partners

▸ Deuchar Park, Morpeth, Northumberland
  NA Sept 1964 p.398

Williamson, R.S. – see entry under Dunham, Widdup & Harrison

Wills, Trenwith & Wills

▸ Buckminster Park, Leicestershire, for Major Tollemache 1965–6
  Robinson 1984 p.204

▸ Fonthill Manor, Tisbury, Wiltshire, for 1st Lord Margadale, 1972–4
  Robinson 1984 pp.77, 209, 211

Wilson, Colin A. St John

▸ Dr Peter Squire house, 2 Grantchester Road, Cambridge, 1963–4

▸ Own house, 2A Grantchester Road, Cambridge, 1963–4
  ABN 7 July 1965 pp.11–15
  AD Nov 1965 pp.546–9
  BM Sept 1966 pp.1037–9
  H&G March 1965 pp.56–9
  Booth & Taylor 1970 pp.191–2
  McKean 1982 p.42
  Listed Grade II

Wilson, Colin A. St John (M.J. Long)

▸ Christopher Cornford house 'Spring House', Conduit Head Road, Cambridge, 1966–7
  ERA May–June 1971 pp.20–21
  Booth & Taylor 1970 pp.194–6
  McKean 1982 p.42
  Listed Grade II

Winter, John

▸ Sheila & Bryan Read house, 21 Upton Close, Norwich, 1956
  Pidgeon & Crosby 1960 pp.104–5
  McKean 1982 p.73

▸ Own house, plus 7 & 9 Regal Lane, London NW1, 1959–61, 1962–3
  BofE London IV p.387

▸ House at Little Bookham, Surrey, 1964

▸ Norma & Alan Day house, Ascot, Berks 1965

▸ Graham & Diana Stewart-Ross house, 1 Bourneside, Wentworth, Surrey, 1965
  AJ 6 June 1966
  Jackson 1996 p.138

▸ Own house, 81 Swain's Lane, London N6, 1969
  AD Aug 1970 pp.420–1
  Ad'A Aug–Sept 1972 pp.26–9
  AJ 26 Aug 1970 pp.465–9
  AJ 28 Oct 1970 pp.1023–4
  Acier Stahl Steel 1971 no.10 pp.390–3
  AJ 25 Oct 1972 pp.968–9
  AJ 22 Nov 1972 pp.1197–8
  McKean & Jestico 1976 p.39
  Jones & Woodward 1992 p.364
  Newton 1992 pp.72–5
  Jackson 1996 pp.138–40

▸ 17a Belsize Lane & 40 Ornan Road, London NW3, 1970
  McKean & Jestico 1976 p.76

Winter, John and Mosse, John

▸ House at Wentworth, Surrey
  AJ 9 Feb 1966 pp.423–8

Winteringham, Graham

▸ Own house, Solihull, Birmingham, c.1960
  Hope 1963 pp.134–7

Wolton, Georgie

▸ Fieldhouse, Crocknorth, Surrey 1969 (demolished and in store)
  Jackson 1996 pp.148–9

▸ Wolton house, Belsize Lane, Belsize Park, 1976
  Newton 1992 pp.88–93

Womersley, Peter

▸ John Womersley house 'Farnley Hey', Farnley Tyas, Huddersfield, W Yorks HD4 6TY, 1954–5
  AR Dec 1955 pp.363–7
  AD March 1956 pp.99–100
  ABN 26 July 1956
  CL 7 Jan 1993 pp.38–41
  H&G Sept 1955 pp.56–8
  BofE Yorks W Riding p.197
  Listed grade II

▸ Womersley house, nr Derwent Canal, Scalby, nr Scarborough, N. Yorks, 1957
  Harling 1961 pp.92–3

▸ Prototype house for builders Murray and Burrel of Galashiels, c.1957
  H&G Dec 1957 pp.73–4

▸ Own house, nr Melrose Abbey, Borders, 1958
  Harling 1961 pp.55–7

▸ House at Ettrick Valley, Galashiels, Borders, c.1960
  Harling 1961 pp.29–31

▸ 2 houses in Rochdale Road East, Ryecroft, Heywood, Manchester, 1960
  Sharp 1966 p.137

▸ Cedar Leys, Alveston, Warwicks, 1964
  D. Hickman Shell Guide

▸ John Womersley house 'Collingwood', Collingwood Hall Drive, Camberley, Surrey, 1962 (demolished)
  AR May 1964 pp.353–4

▸ House at Turnberry, Ayrshire, 1963
  Whiting 1964 pp.84–90
  Willis 1977 p.10

▸ House at Fletcher Moss Park, Didsbury, Manchester, 1964

▸ Womersley house, Bath, 1968
  IH Oct 1972 pp.39–45
  BB Jan 1973 pp.3–9

Wood, Kenneth

▸ Wildwood, Oxshott, Surrey, 1957–9
  Harling 1961 pp.66–7
  BofE Surrey p.401

▸ Vincent House, Warren Road, Kingston upon Thames, 1959
  AR November 1961 pp.343–44
  CL 7 June 1962 pp.1383–5
  Nairn 1964 p.105

▸ Fenwycks, Tekels Avenue, Camberley, Surrey, 1960
  BofE Surrey p.128

▸ Stanley Picker house, 1 Warren Park, Kingswood, Kingston upon Thames, 1965–8
  BofE Surrey p.336; London 2, p.320

Woodward, Geoffrey

▸ House at Hertingfordbury, Herts, 1955
  Walter 1955/7 pp.72–3
  Clifford 1957 pp.124–5

Wright, John

▸ House at Draycott Place, Chelsea, London SW3
  AR Aug 1968 p.112

Wroughton, H.J. and B.P.

▶ Own house, Moles Hill, Surrey, 1953
Clifford 1957 p.127

Yakely, Stephen & Associates

▶ House at 21 Horn Lane, Linton,
Cambs, 1971
McKean 1982 p.43

▶ House at 49 Mingle Lane, Stapleford,
Cambs, 1971
McKean 1982 p.44

Yorke, Harper & Harvey –
see Harvey, Robert

Yorke, Francis Reginald Stevens, Rosenberg, Eugene, and Mardall, Cyril S. (F.R.S. Yorke)

▶ The New House, Luccombe,
Shanklin, IoW, 1946–7
AJ 13 Feb 1947 pp.167–9
'Zinc Bulletin' 4, Spring 1948
Penn 1954 p.153
YRM 1972 p.122
Emanuel 1980 p.912
Powers 1992

Yorke, Rosenberg and Mardall, (with Corr and McCormick)

▶ Dr Cole house, Londonderry,
Northern Ireland, 1951
YRM 1972 p.122
Emanuel 1980 p.913

Yorke, Rosenberg and Mardall

▶ House at Connaught Mews, London
W2, c.1951–2
AJ 29 Jan 1953
H&G Sept 1952 pp.58–9, 78
Penn 1954 p.25, 90–1

▶ (F.R.S. Yorke)
Own house conversion 'The Mill',
Wootton, Oxon, 1953
Penn 1954 p.60
YRM 1972 p.123

▶ Boxgrove Houses Ltd prototype,
George Road, Coombe, 1956
YRM 1972 p.123

▶ Wootton Rectory for Rev Struan
Robertson, Wootton, Oxford, 1956
YRM 1972 p.123

▶ Dr Jacobus house, Jack Straws Lane,
Oxford, 1956
YRM 1972 p.123

▶ Philip Harben house, 115 Great
George Street, London SW1, 1957
YRM 1972 p.123

▶ J. Spedan Lewis house, Longstock,
Hants, 1959
YRM 1972 p.124

▶ N.J. Payne house, Shamley Green,
Surrey, 1961
YRM 1972 p.124

▶ D. Keddie house 'Ark House',
ʌhford, Essex, 1962–4
ˑq 1964 pp.48–51
˙ᵔ p.124
ᵔᵔ p.132

ᵔns)
ᵛ Green, Bucks, 1963
ᵏ6

▶ (Brian Henderson)
Own guest pavilion, Great Bedwyn,
Wilts, c.1970

▶ (David Allford)
Own House at Pewsey, Wilts, c.1970

Youngman, John

▶ Youngman House, 1 Wilberforce
Road, Cambridge, 1965
Booth & Taylor 1970 p.193

Yuille, Bill, of Burnet, Tait & Partners

▶ Own house, 6 Bacon's Lane,
London N6, 1955